D1272522

Fast & Funny
Paper Toys You Can Make

••••••

E. Richard Churchill

Illustrated by James Michaels

Sterling Publishing Co., Inc.   New York

To Chum, with love

Special thanks to the students of Brentwood Middle School, Greeley, Colorado, for coming up with great ideas.

Edited by Timothy Nolan

Library of Congress Cataloging-in-Publication Data
Churchill, E. Richard (Elmer Richard)
    Fast and funny paper toys you can make / by E. Richard Churchill.
        p.   cm.
    Includes index.
    Summary: Directions for making from household articles paper toys
    that move. Includes boats, noisemakers, puppets, mobiles, and more.
    ISBN 0-8069-5770-0
    1. Paper toy making—Juvenile literature. [1. Paper toy making.
    2. Toy making. 3. Handicraft.] I. Title.
    TT174.5.P3C47 1989
745.592—dc20   89-32411
                                                      CIP
                                                      AC

10 9 8 7 6 5 4 3 2 1

First paperback edition published in 1991 by
Sterling Publishing Company, Inc.
387 Park Avenue South, New York, N.Y. 10016
© 1989 by E. Richard Churchill
Distributed in Canada by Sterling Publishing
% Canadian Manda Group, P.O. Box 920, Station U
Toronto, Ontario, Canada M8Z 5P9
Distributed in Great Britain and Europe by Cassell PLC
Villiers House, 41/47 Strand, London WC2N 5JE, England
Distributed in Australia by Capricorn Ltd.
P.O. Box 665, Lane Cove, NSW 2066
Manufactured in the United States of America
All rights reserved

Sterling ISBN 0-8069-5770-0   Trade
              0-8069-5771-9   Paper

Contents

Before You Begin

All the paper toys in this book move. The boats all float, the noisy toys all create sounds, the puppets come alive. Mobiles turn, spinners spin, balancing toys balance, and tumblers tumble. The games all have moving parts to make them fun.

These toys use things you already have around the house like notebook paper, cereal boxes, and milk cartons.

Don't feel that you have to begin on the first page and make each moving paper toy in order. Jump around if you wish. Have fun with these moving paper toys.

Some toys you can build in a few seconds. Others take lots more time. Just follow the directions and don't get in a great hurry, and you can make and enjoy every toy in this book.

METRIC EQUIVALENCY CHART

MM—MILLIMETRES   CM—CENTIMETRES

INCHES TO MILLIMETRES AND CENTIMETRES

INCHES	MM	CM	INCHES	CM	INCHES	CM
⅛	3	0.3	9	22.9	30	76.2
¼	6	0.6	10	25.4	31	78.7
⅜	10	1.0	11	27.9	32	81.3
½	13	1.3	12	30.5	33	83.8
⅝	16	1.6	13	33.0	34	86.4
¾	19	1.9	14	35.6	35	88.9
⅞	22	2.2	15	38.1	36	91.4
1	25	2.5	16	40.6	37	94.0
1¼	32	3.2	17	43.2	38	96.5
1½	38	3.8	18	45.7	39	99.1
1¾	44	4.4	19	48.3	40	101.6
2	51	5.1	20	50.8	41	104.1
2½	64	6.4	21	53.3	42	106.7
3	76	7.6	22	55.9	43	109.2
3½	89	8.9	23	58.4	44	111.8
4	102	10.2	24	61.0	45	114.3
4½	114	11.4	25	63.5	46	116.8
5	127	12.7	26	66.0	47	119.4
6	152	15.2	27	68.6	48	121.9
7	178	17.8	28	71.1	49	124.5
8	203	20.3	29	73.7	50	127.0

YARDS TO METRES

YARDS	METRES	YARDS	METRES	YARDS	METRES	YARDS	METRES	YARDS	METRES
⅛	0.11	2⅛	1.94	4⅛	3.77	6⅛	5.60	8⅛	7.43
¼	0.23	2¼	2.06	4¼	3.89	6¼	5.72	8¼	7.54
⅜	0.34	2⅜	2.17	4⅜	4.00	6⅜	5.83	8⅜	7.66
½	0.46	2½	2.29	4½	4.11	6½	5.94	8½	7.77
⅝	0.57	2⅝	2.40	4⅝	4.23	6⅝	6.06	8⅝	7.89
¾	0.69	2¾	2.51	4¾	4.34	6¾	6.17	8¾	8.00
⅞	0.80	2⅞	2.63	4⅞	4.46	6⅞	6.29	8⅞	8.12
1	0.91	3	2.74	5	4.57	7	6.40	9	8.23
1⅛	1.03	3⅛	2.86	5⅛	4.69	7⅛	6.52	9⅛	8.34
1¼	1.14	3¼	2.97	5¼	4.80	7¼	6.63	9¼	8.46
1⅜	1.26	3⅜	3.09	5⅜	4.91	7⅜	6.74	9⅜	8.57
1½	1.37	3½	3.20	5½	5.03	7½	6.86	9½	8.69
1⅝	1.49	3⅝	3.31	5⅝	5.14	7⅝	6.97	9⅝	8.80
1¾	1.60	3¾	3.43	5¾	5.26	7¾	7.09	9¾	8.92
1⅞	1.71	3⅞	3.54	5⅞	5.37	7⅞	7.20	9⅞	9.03
2	1.83	4	3.66	6	5.49	8	7.32	10	9.14

· 1 ·
Sailing, Sailing

Soap Boat

No, this boat is not made from a bar of soap. It gets its power from liquid soap.

A piece of milk carton material is perfect for this project. Cut out a piece 3 inches by 2 inches from the side of the carton. Draw the outline in Illus. 1; then cut out your Soap Boat.

Place the boat in a tub or sink of water. Don't fill the tub to the top. All that this boat needs is about ½ inch of water in which to float.

Put a little bit of liquid dish soap at the spot shown by the circle in Illus. 2. Watch your Soap Boat take off across the water.

When the bit of soap is used up, your boat will come to a stop. Add another dab of liquid soap and it will take off again.

Once the surface of the water gets a film of soap, your boat will no longer move. When that happens, just drain the water, refill the sink, and start over again.

Milk carton material is best for your Soap Boat since it is waterproofed to hold liquid. If you use cereal box material you can use crayons to color the underside of the boat.

Illus. 3 has some Soap Boat designs you may want to try. You can also try some designs of your own.

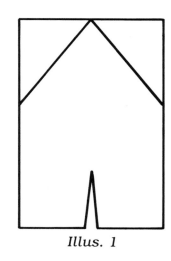

Illus. 1

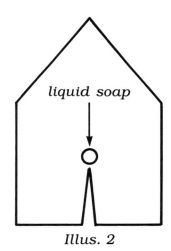

liquid soap

Illus. 2

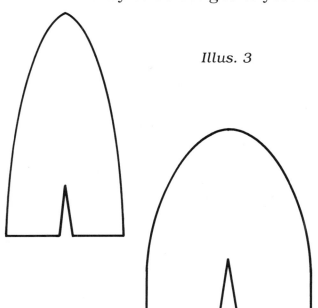

Illus. 3

7

Little Fellow

The side of a milk carton is perfect for making Little Fellow. The plastic-foam hamburger containers some of the fast-food places use work fine, too.

Illus. 4

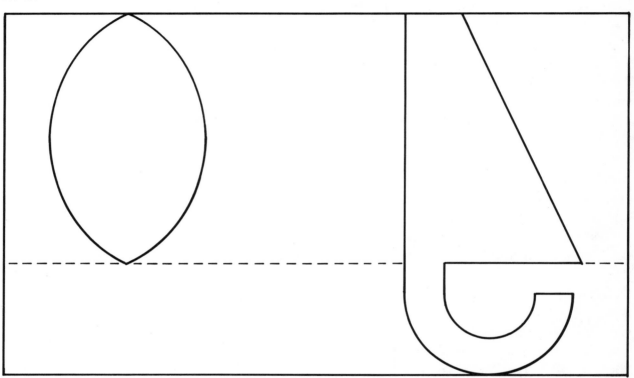

Sketch the two pieces in Illus. 4. The pieces do not have to be exactly 2¾ inches and 4 inches, but try to come close to these sizes. What is important is that the height of the sail be exactly the same as the length of the hull, which is the part of the boat touching the water.

Cut out the two pieces; then, very carefully, make a 1-inch slit in the middle of the hull, as in Illus. 5.

Remember that the coated material of which milk cartons are made is quite tough, so don't poke the table or your finger. Just use slow, steady pressure and keep your fingers out of the way!

Illus. 5

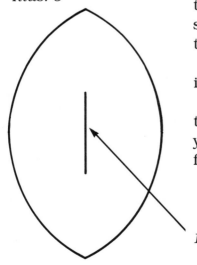

1" cut

Slip the bottom of the sail section through the slit as in Illus. 6. Insert the end marked with the "X" and carefully push the hull around the curve until it comes to the bottom of the sail.

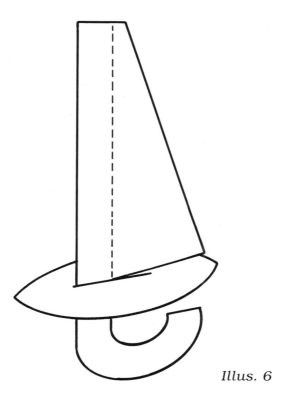

Illus. 6

Put the two parts together to form Little Fellow. The part of the boat below the hull is called the keel. It keeps the boat upright and sailing forward.

Bend the sail just a bit along the dotted line in Illus. 6, and place it in the sink or tub. Give a little puff of air on the sail and watch it move away from you.

If you want to build other Little Fellows, think about changing the size of the hull and making the sail a little wider than in your first model. A large sail and narrow hull make a sailboat move faster. Just don't get too much sail area or too small a hull, or your Little Fellow will end up on its side.

Easy Float

To make the Easy Float you need to start with a square piece of paper. Waxed paper is best since it is waterproof. Aluminum kitchen foil works fine, too, but be careful when you fold it.

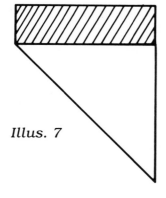

If you want to use notebook or typing paper, you can waterproof it by coloring one side with crayons. You can either color all of one side before you begin folding or wait and color just the hull after you fold the boat. Either way works just fine.

Illus. 7

Since notebook and typing paper is rectangular, here's how to make it into a square. Fold one corner of the paper over as in Illus. 7. Cut off the shaded part. When you unfold the paper, you have a square. Remember this for other projects.

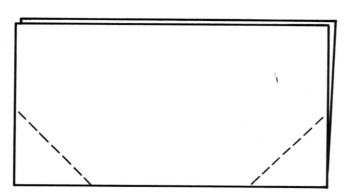

Illus. 8

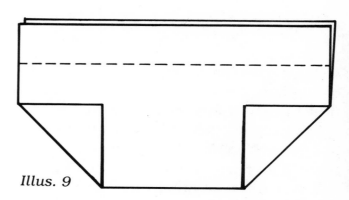

Illus. 9

Now, fold the paper in half as in Illus. 8. The dotted lines show the next folds. Fold the two corners over so that your material looks like Illus. 9. Crease these folds by running your thumbnail over them.

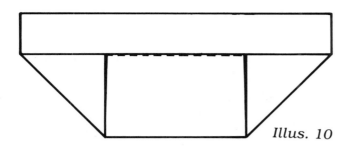

Illus. 10

The dotted line in Illus. 9 is actually two folds. Fold the top layer of paper towards you; then turn the paper over and repeat this fold with the second side, so that your boat looks like Illus. 10. Naturally, the dotted line tells where to make your final fold.

Once again, fold the top layer of paper towards you; then turn the paper over and fold the bottom layer. The finished boat is shown in Illus. 11.

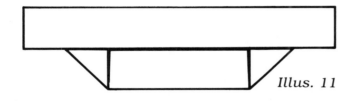

Illus. 11

Open the top of the boat by separating the two sides. Push up on the bottom of the hull a bit to make the hull flat on the bottom. This will keep it from tipping over in the water.

Give your folded boat a little cargo to provide it with enough weight in the bottom of the hull so that it can float properly. Give it a small shove to send it on its way.

You will be surprised at how much cargo this folded boat can carry. Just for fun see how many paper clips or marbles it can hold without sinking.

Foil Hull Boat

The lid from any small box and some aluminum foil make a boat that is quick and easy to construct. Wrap a layer of aluminum foil around the outside of the box lid. Bend the foil up along each side and tuck it in at the top. Crimp the foil in at the corners to hold it in place, and your Foil Hull Boat looks like Illus. 12.

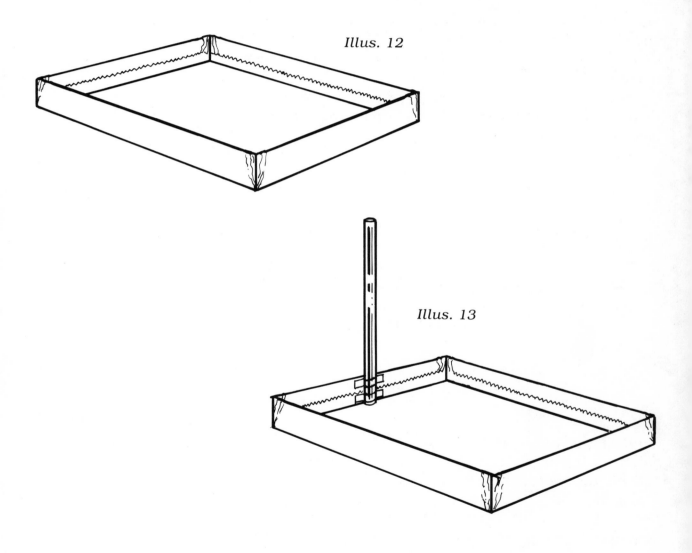

Illus. 12

Illus. 13

Now, how about a sail? First, we need a mast. A plastic drinking straw is great if you have one handy. Just tape it in place on the front side of the box as shown in Illus. 13.

If you don't have a plastic straw, you can make a mast quite easily. Cut a sheet of notebook paper in half, and roll it up tightly. To keep it from unrolling, use two or three bits of transparent tape as in Illus. 14.

The sail is simple. It size depends upon the side box or box lid you used for the hull. The larger the box or lid, the larger the sail.

Poke two small holes in the sail as shown in Illus. 15; then slip the sail onto the mast. Your Foil Hull Boat should look like the one in Illus. 16.

This boat won't win a lot of races, but it will carry quite a bit of cargo.

If you don't have any aluminum foil, try plastic kitchen wrap. Instead of crimping the corners to hold it in place, use some short pieces of transparent tape instead.

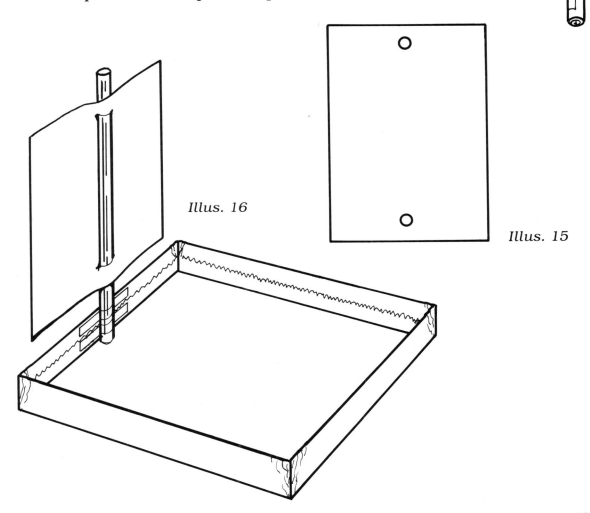

Illus. 14

Tape ⟶

Illus. 16

Illus. 15

Balloon-Powered Boat

A milk carton, a balloon, and a plastic drinking straw make a great little power boat. The quart or half-gallon size milk carton is best for this project.

Cut one side off the milk carton, as in Illus. 17. Poke a hole in the stern, or back, of the boat about ¼ inch from the bottom. Illus. 18 shows this. Be careful and remember how tough milk cartons are and how tender fingers are. Make the hole just large enough for the straw.

Illus. 17

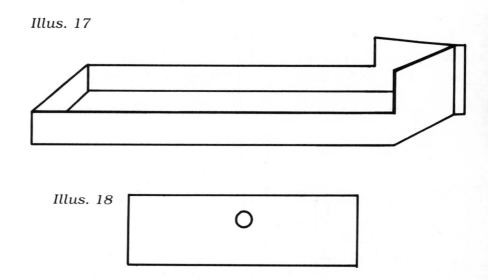

Illus. 18

A balloon can't push water!

Oh, yeah?

14

Push one end of the plastic straw into the opening of a balloon. Wrap a rubber band around the balloon's opening several times, as in Illus. 19. The rubber band has to be tight enough to keep the balloon on the straw but not so tight that it collapses the straw. If the band is too tight, you will blow your brains out trying to inflate the balloon.

Place the balloon in the boat so that the end of the plastic straw sticks out through the hole you made. Blow up the balloon through the end of the straw. Your boat will look like Illus. 20.

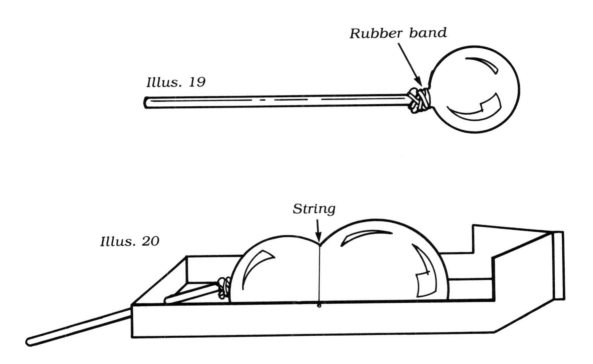

Rubber band

Illus. 19

String

Illus. 20

If the balloon slips out of the boat, use a short piece of string as a safety belt, as in Illus. 20. This probably won't be needed but takes just a minute to install if your balloon is hard to deal with.

The Balloon-Powered Boat makes great motor boat putt-putt sounds as the air escapes from the balloon and pushes the boat forward. As the balloon loses its air the end of the straw in the water may want to come to the surface. When that happens the escaping air no longer powers the boat. To prevent this, use a piece of tape inside the boat's stern to fasten the straw securely at an angle.

Plate Boat

Just a minute's work will turn a plastic-foam plate into a pretty neat little bathtub boat. (A paper plate won't work because—well, think about it.)

He went down with his paper!

Cut the plate in half along the dotted line in Illus. 21. Cut 1¼ inches off each of the halves. The dotted line in Illus. 22 shows this cut. Save these strips. You'll use them in just a minute.

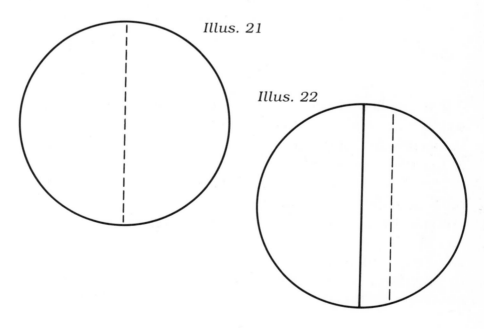

Illus. 21

Illus. 22

Place the two plate pieces together. Tape them firmly as shown in Illus. 23. Masking tape is great since it is fairly waterproof, but any tape will do the job. Tape both sides just to make sure this seam holds.

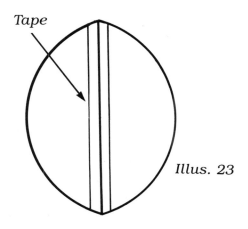

Tape

Illus. 23

Now use the strips of material to make a seat. (Use one or both, whichever you want.) Cut the strips to the proper length, and use either tape or staples to attach the seat or seats to the sides of the boat. This also makes the boat stronger. Illus. 24 shows your finished Plate Boat.

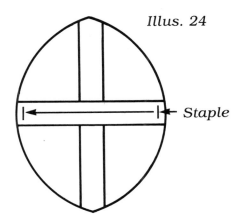

Illus. 24

Staple

After you have floated the Plate Boat you may want to turn it into a balloon-powered craft. This makes the boat more interesting and takes only a few seconds.

Poke a hole in the bottom of the boat as shown by the circle in Illus. 25. Don't make this hole any larger than necessary for a plastic drinking straw to slip through. You don't want a leaking boat!

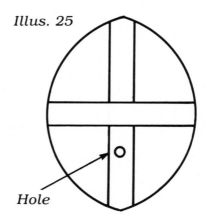

Illus. 25

Hole

Use a straw and balloon just as you did for the balloon-powered boat you made from a milk carton. Remember not to wrap the rubber band too tightly around the balloon's mouth or the straw will squeeze shut. Illus. 26 shows the straw and balloon in place and ready to go.

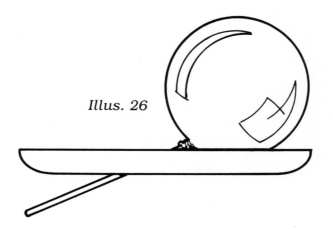

Illus. 26

If the boat does not sail straight, it may be because the straw isn't extending straight back into the water. If this happens, you need a rudder.

Cut a rudder out of a piece of milk carton or use one of the ends left over from the seats. It does not have to be fancy to work, but it should match Illus. 27 in order to work.

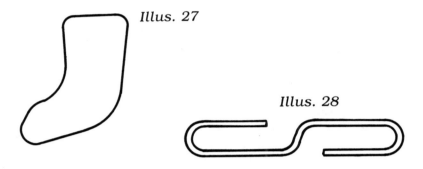

Illus. 27

Illus. 28

Bend a paper clip open the long way so that it looks like Illus. 28. Poke one end of the clip through the stern. Use a short piece of tape to fasten the rudder to the part of the paper clip which extends over the boat's stern. Now the rudder can help control the direction your boat sails.

To hold the rudder firm, use a second piece of tape inside the boat as in Illus. 29. To adjust the rudder, just loosen the tape a bit and turn it to its new position.

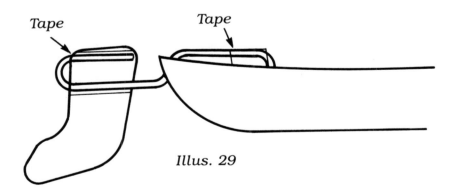

Tape

Tape

Illus. 29

Folded Catamaran

A catamaran is a boat with twin hulls. The two hulls make it very stable and hard to turn over in the water.

To fold this boat, start with a square piece of waterproof paper. Fold the paper diagonally both ways and unfold it. This helps locate the center of the paper. The folds are shown by the dotted lines in Illus. 30.

Illus. 30

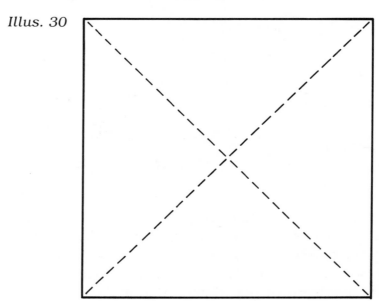

Now fold all four corners in to the middle. Crease these folds into place with your thumbnail, and your catamaran looks like Illus. 31.

Illus. 31

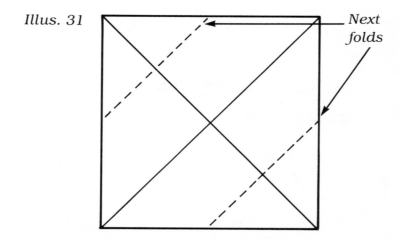

Next folds

The two dotted lines in Illus. 31 show your next folds. These folds are made so that the points finish up on the back of the paper. Turn the paper over and fold the two points in so that they meet at the center; then turn the paper back over. It looks like Illus. 32 now.

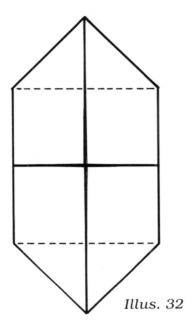

Illus. 32

The dotted lines in Illus. 32 indicate the next folds you will be making. This time fold the two points forward. The completed folds are in Illus. 33.

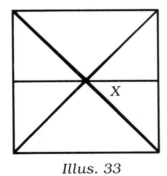

Illus. 33

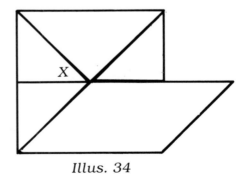

Illus. 34

The "X" in Illus. 33 shows where to begin the next step. Take hold of that point and gently pull so that it unfolds and turns into what you see in Illus. 34.

The "X" in Illus. 34 shows the next point to pull out in the same manner. When this is done you have reached Illus. 35.

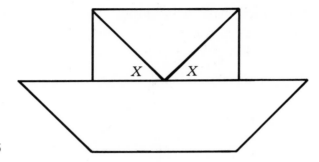

Illus. 35

The two "X"s in Illus. 35 show where to pull out the final two points just as you have already done. When these points are pulled into place, your catamaran-to-be is shown in Illus. 36.

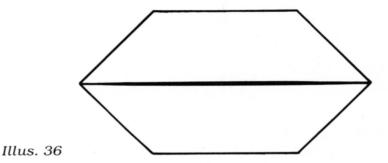

Illus. 36

All that remains is to fold the two halves of the boat by folding the project down its central fold. Spread the two parts of the boat open and the finished boat is seen in Illus. 37.

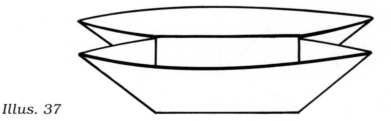

Illus. 37

This little fellow does just fine in a sink or bathtub. If it gets waterlogged let it dry out, and it'll be ready to sail again.

Center Wheel Paddle Boat

It is not very difficult to turn a plastic-foam plate into a paddle boat. If the plate is thin, you may need to use two to give your Center Wheel Paddle Boat strength.

Cut the center out of the plate. The cut should be about ½ inch inside the crease already in the plate. Illus. 38 shows the plate with its center removed.

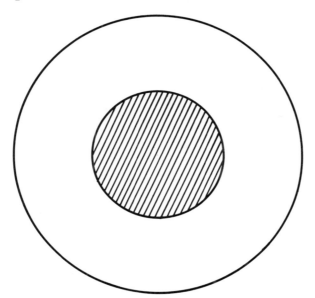

Illus. 38

If you have thin plates you will probably need to cut the centers from two of them. Use masking tape or transparent tape to fasten them together. Wrap a length of tape around the two plates as shown in Illus. 39.

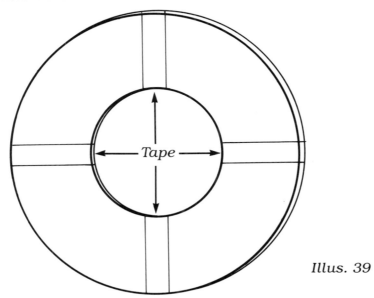

Tape

Illus. 39

Now you need two paper clips and a rubber band. Slip the clips over the ends of the rubber band as in Illus. 40.

Illus. 40

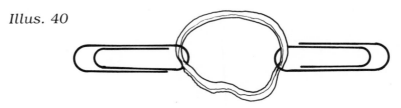

Poke a little hole in each side of the plate about ½ inch from the inside edge. These holes are shown in Illus. 41.

Slip the outer edge of the paper clips through these holes, so that your paddle boat looks like Illus. 42.

Illus. 41

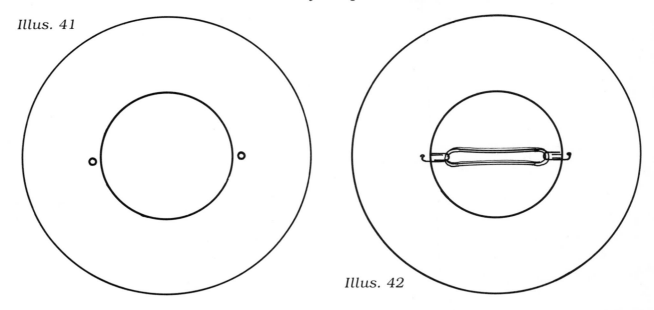

Illus. 42

Making a paddle wheel is easy. Just cut a piece of milk carton about 2 × 3 inches. Fold it in half the long way to form a double thickness of material 1 × 3 inches. Staple or tape it along the open edge, as in Illus. 43, so that it does not unfold.

Staples

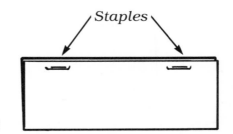

Illus. 43

Slip the paddle between the two sides of the rubber band and begin turning it. Once the rubber band is twisted tightly (or you are tired of turning the paddle), it is time to test your boat.

Launch it in the bathtub and see what it does. When the rubber band completely unwinds, rewind it and get ready for another voyage.

If you want to put a rudder on this boat, make it just like the rudder on the other Plate Boat. It only takes a minute. When you install your boat's rudder, remember to place it in line with the paddle. Don't put the rudder on the same side as one of the paper clips because it won't have any effect there.

Experiment with larger paddles or even two rubber bands hooked between the paper clips for more power. If one of the paper clips happens to pull out, don't throw the boat away. Just make a new hole for the clip and your paddle boat is as good as new.

Just be careful who you meet on the boat!

Milk Carton Paddle Boat

This paddle boat is a stern wheeler. This means the paddle is located at the stern of the boat.

Either a quart- or a half-gallon carton will make a good paddle boat. Cut half of the carton away as in Illus. 44. Whether you leave the windscreen in front is up to you, but don't throw away the part of the carton you remove. You'll need it later.

Illus. 44

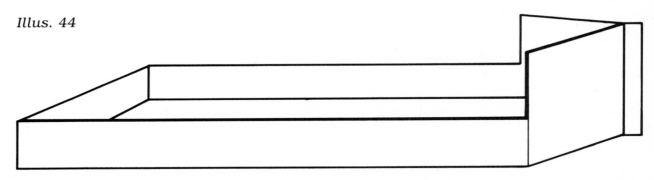

Cut a 2 × 3-inch piece of milk carton material. Double it to form a piece 1 × 3 inches. Use two staples to hold it together as in Illus. 45. This is your paddle.

Next, take two 8 × 4-inch pieces of material. Fold each of them in thirds the long way. The dotted lines in Illus. 46 show these folds. Use two staples to hold the folded material together. Be sure to place the staples in about the same locations as they are in Illus. 47.

Staples

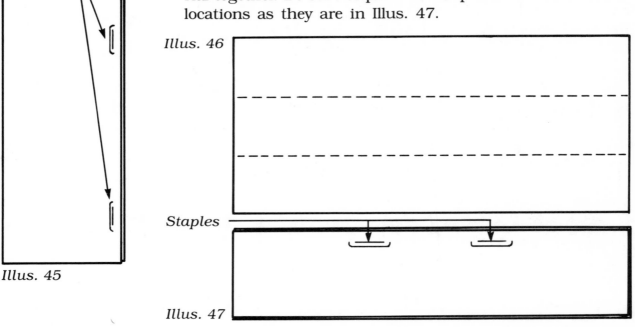

Illus. 45

Illus. 46

Staples

Illus. 47

Just one more piece of material is needed. It should be 6 × 2 inches. Fold it into thirds the long way just as you did the larger pieces of cardboard, and staple it the same way.

Now you are ready to put the Milk Carton Paddle Boat together.

Illus. 48

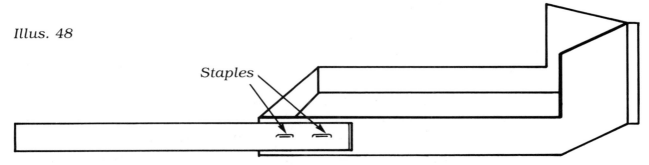

Staples

Take the two larger folded pieces of cardboard. Hold one so that it overlaps the side of the boat by about 2½ inches. Staple it into place with two staples. Illus. 48 shows it stapled into position. Do the same with the second piece of large material on the opposite side of the boat.

Fold the ends of the remaining piece up so that it looks like a big letter U. The bottom of the U should be ½ inch wider than the boat's stern. Illus. 49 shows this.

Slip the ends of this piece into the centers of the two pieces of cardboard stapled to the boat's stern. Push the crosspiece in as far as it will go; then use a staple to hold it in place. Illus. 50 shows a top view of the paddle boat with the crosspiece already stapled into position.

Slip a rubber band around the two chunks of cardboard which extend back from the stern. Illus. 51 shows the rubber band in its proper position.

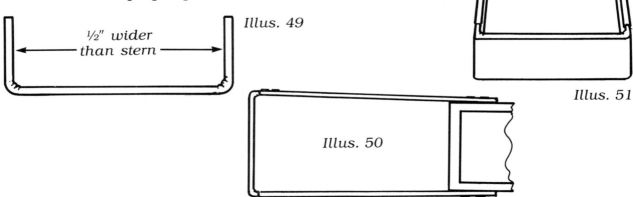

½" wider than stern

Illus. 49

Illus. 50

Illus. 51

Slip the paddle between the two sides of the rubber band and begin twisting. Turn the paddle backwards as you twist. This way, when you release the paddle it will push forward. When you have given it twenty or thirty twists, launch your paddle boat for its first test sailing.

If you happen to turn the paddle in the wrong direction, the boat will move backwards. Just twist the paddle in the opposite direction.

Experiment with how tightly you can twist the rubber band before it causes the braces to begin to bow in. You can make the braces stronger by using a bit more material in them and making them four or five folds thick. When you do this, you run into trouble stapling them onto the boat itself, so don't try to make them too thick.

Your Milk Carton Paddle Boat is a good bathtub sailer which can sail empty or carry quite a bit of cargo.

· 2 ·
Noisy Toys

Paper Popper

You will need a 6-inch square of really stiff paper for your popper. Lightweight cardboard is best. The side of a cereal box works great. So does a square cut from a file folder or heavy construction paper. You also need a small square of lighter paper. A 4-inch square of notebook paper is fine.

Fold both squares diagonally. This leaves them looking like Illus. 52. Set the larger square aside for just a minute.

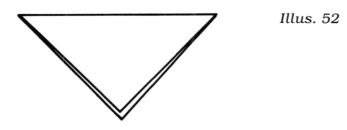

Illus. 52

Cut off one corner of the smaller square as shown in Illus. 53. A ½-inch cut is perfect.

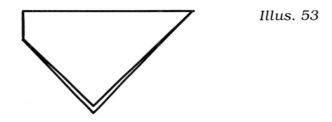

Illus. 53

Now unfold the paper. It should look like Illus. 54. The dotted lines show where to fold the two sides up. Crease these folds; then unfold the paper.

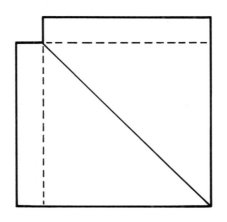

Illus. 54

Now you need the larger square. Lay it flat so that the fold faces up. Place the smaller square on top of it as in Illus. 55.

Illus. 55

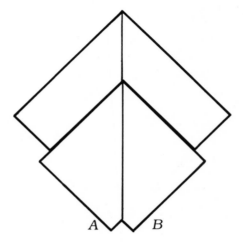

Fold flaps A and B around the larger square. Illus. 56 shows the rear view of the popper with the flaps folded over. Use two strips of transparent tape as shown in the drawing to fasten the two parts of the popper together. Glue will work just as well as tape, but be sure to let it dry before using your popper.

Illus. 56

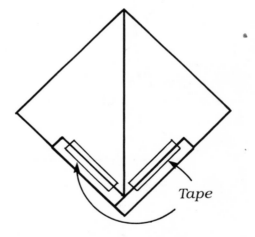

Tape

To make your popper pop, fold the larger square together. The smaller square will fold right up inside the big one. Hold the heavy piece of material firmly between your thumb and finger. Be sure you are holding the end opposite the taped flaps, and that the folded edge of the large square points up. Illus. 57 shows how.

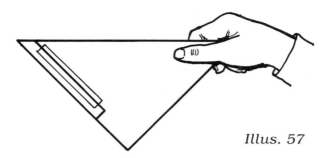

Illus. 57

Snap your hand down quickly. If everything is working properly, the smaller paper will unfold with a loud popping noise. If it does not unfold—try again! If the popper still does not unfold and pop, make sure that the end of the popper you are not holding can spread apart a bit to let the paper slip out. Sometimes the really stiff sides don't spread the first few times. When it pops, just fold the smaller square back into place. Once you have the hang of it, there is nothing more fun than making all sorts of noise with your popper.

After you have popped a number of times, the smaller paper will probably get a rip in it. When that happens, just peel it off the heavy square and make another small square. This way, your popper will last for hundreds of loud pops.

Experiment with different-sized smaller squares and different types of paper. When you find just the right size and type of paper you are really in the popper business, at least until someone gets tired of all the noise!

I never get tired of this!

Quick Paper Popper

It takes about thirty seconds to fold this popper that you can use time and time again.

Begin with a square piece of paper. Notebook or typing paper is ideal. Fold it diagonally so that your paper looks like Illus. 58. The dotted line shows your next fold.

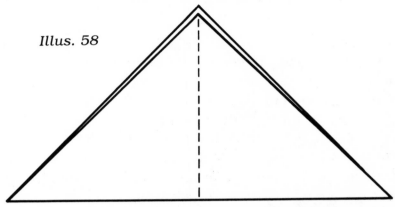

Illus. 58

Fold the paper along the dotted line in Illus. 58 and crease that fold. Your Quick Paper Popper is now like Illus. 59.

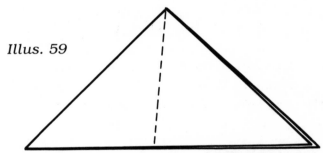

Illus. 59

Look carefully at the dotted line in Illus. 59. Notice that it does not run directly down the middle of the paper. It angles off to one side.

Fold only the top layer of your paper over at an angle so that a little tail of paper sticks out as in Illus. 60.

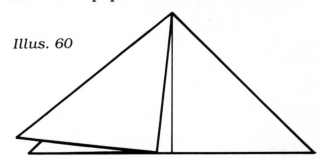

Illus. 60

Turn the paper over and fold the second side so that it matches the first. The two little tails of paper should be exactly the same, and look like Illus. 61.

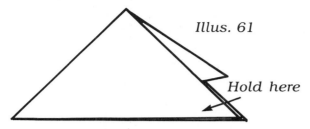

Illus. 61

Hold here

Grasp the popper firmly between your thumb and forefinger so that you are holding both little paper tails tightly. The arrow in Illus. 61 shows where to grab hold.

Snap your hand and wrist down sharply. The middle of the popper should fly out with a loud popping sound.

Push the middle of the popper back into place and pop it again. Do this as long as you wish or until the popper tears.

Don't worry about mending a torn popper. Just make a new one.

After you have popped this popper enough times to know how it performs, make a larger popper. Use a sheet of newspaper and see what sort of sound it makes. The advertising sections in many newspapers make dandy paper poppers.

Whirling Hummer

This noisy toy makes a humming sound as it spins through the air.

Cut three rectangular pieces out of cereal boxes. Make each piece 4 × 6 inches. Cut the centers out of all three pieces so that they look like Illus. 62. Leave 1 inch all the way around each rectangle when you cut out the centers.

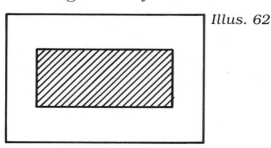

Illus. 62

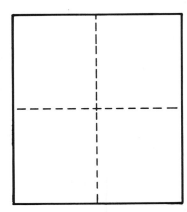

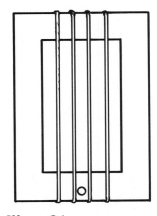

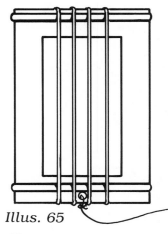

Glue the three pieces of material together so that they form a rectangle three layers thick. This will make them good and stiff.

While the glue is drying, cut a sheet of notebook paper into four rectangles. The dotted lines in Illus. 63 show how.

Now roll each of the four pieces of notebook paper into a tight roll. Roll along the short side so that you end up with a 4-inch-wide tube. A piece of transparent tape will hold the four tubes together.

When the glue is dry on the layered rectangle, place four rubber bands around it as shown in Illus. 64. It is the vibration of these rubber bands that will make this toy hum.

Very carefully poke the hole in the cardboard shown in Illus. 64. The cardboard is three layers thick and quite tough, so don't make a hole in your finger or the desk or table. A thick layer of newspaper or cardboard should help protect you.

Cut a piece of string about 3 feet long. Tie one end very securely through the hole you just made, and make a loop in the other end of the string about 1 inch across.

Slip the rolled tubes of paper under the rubber bands so that two tubes are on each side of the cardboard. Push the tubes as far as you can towards the ends of the cardboard. Illus. 65 shows the tubes in place. The other two tubes are on the opposite side of the cardboard.

Now go outside and test your Whirling Hummer. Slip the loop in the string over your forefinger and clench your fist. Make sure you are a safe distance (at least 5 feet) from people, windows, buildings, and anything else.

Spin the hummer above your head. The faster it spins, the better it hums. Change its tone by spinning it faster or slower.

Experiment by adding or removing rubber bands. Try the hummer without the paper tubes in place or with only two tubes. Use a longer string to change the speed your hummer spins.

Always use this toy outside and don't hit anything!

Hummer Two

The tube from a toilet-tissue roll is just right to make Hummer Two. A small soft-drink cup is also fine.

Make two cuts ⅜ inch or ½ inch apart as in Illus. 66. Bend the narrow strip of cardboard between the cuts up and cut it off.

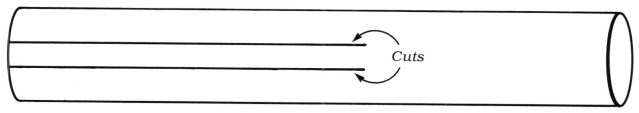

Cuts

Illus. 66

If your soft-drink cup has a lid, press it down tightly on top. If not, then take a piece of stiff material (such as a file card) and draw around one end of the tube. Cut the card about ¾ inch larger than the circle. Illus. 67 shows this.

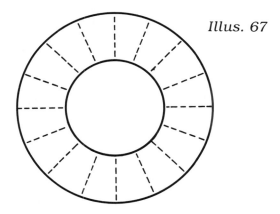

Illus. 67

All the dotted lines in Illus. 67 are cuts to make so that you can fold the edges of the card down around the tube or cut.

It said Hummer, not stumbler!

Place this card or stiff paper on the end of the tube and fold down all the little loose ends so that it looks like Illus. 68. Tape the loose ends down firmly. Use short pieces of tape and tape only three or four ends at a time. Otherwise, you may need four hands to do the job.

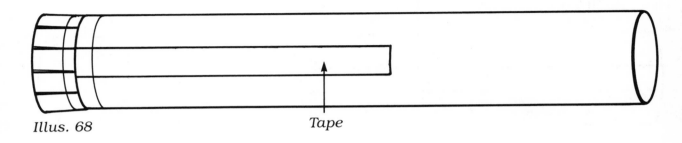

Illus. 68

Tape

Illus. 69

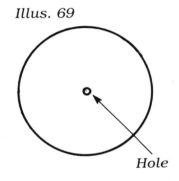

Hole

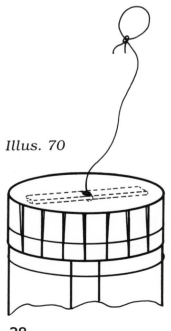

Illus. 70

Poke a little hole in the end as in Illus. 69.

Now cut about 3 feet of string and break a toothpick or a matchstick off so that it is about 1 inch long. Push one end of the string through the hole you poked in the file card, and pull it down so that it sticks out the other end of the tube. If you are using a soft-drink cup, work the string's end out the side of the cut through the slit in the side.

Tie that end of the string around the middle of the toothpick or matchstick. Pull the other end of the string until the stick rests right against the underside of the file card, as in Illus. 70.

Now tie a loop in the other end of the string, about 1 inch across. Slip that loop over your finger and clench your fist.

Now go outside and spin Hummer Two around and around over your head. Remember to stand in an open area.

It should reward all your hard work with a nice humming sound.

Experiment by spinning Hummer Two faster or slower. Try cutting the bottom out of the cup, or making the slit in the side of the tube a little wider. Just be careful with your scissors. Try a smaller hole by putting a small piece of tape over part of the cut. See how the hummer sounds then.

Outlandish

Words simply do not describe the noise this makes.

Begin with a square sheet of notebook paper. Turn it so that one of the corners points directly at you, as in Illus. 71. Roll it into a round tube ¼ inch across. (A good way to do this is to roll the paper around a pencil.) Use a little piece of transparent tape to keep the loose end from unrolling. The roll should look like Illus. 72.

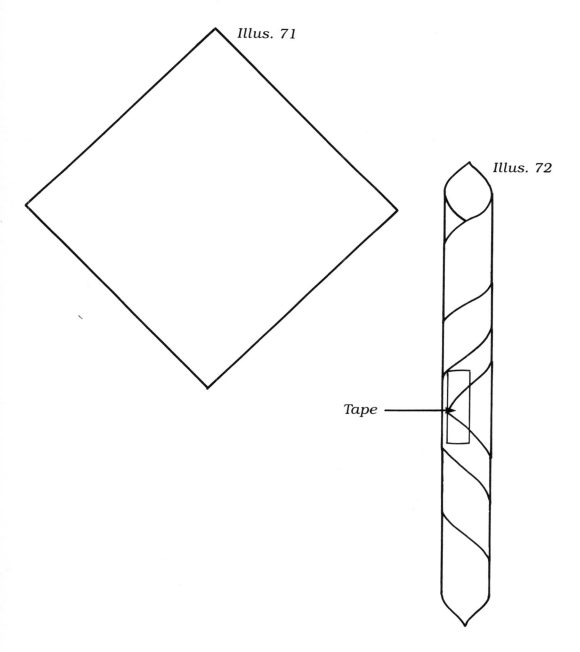

Illus. 71

Illus. 72

Tape

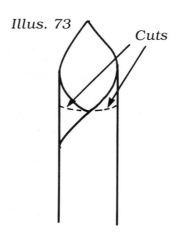

Illus. 73   *Cuts*

Illus. 73 shows one end of the rolled paper. The dotted lines show two cuts to make. Be very careful making these cuts—they should be only about ¼ inch long.

After making the two cuts, fold the little triangle of paper up so that it fits over the opening at the end of the rolled paper. It looks like Illus. 74.

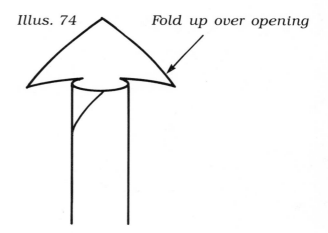

Illus. 74   *Fold up over opening*

Place the uncut end of the tube in your mouth and inhale. Don't blow. As you suck air in, it will cause the little triangle of paper to flutter or vibrate against the rest of the rolled tube. The sounds it creates will be unlike anything you have heard before.

Experiment until you discover exactly how hard to suck in. If you inhale too hard, the paper will stick against the tube and you will turn red from trying to pull air past it. If you don't inhale hard enough, the triangle of paper won't vibrate and you won't get a sound.

Tube Hummer

The Tube Hummer is another noisy toy that moves through vibration.

To make this toy you need a cardboard tube like the one in the middle of a roll of wrapping paper. A 10- or 12-inch tube is best. If you don't have a tube handy, make one from cereal box material.

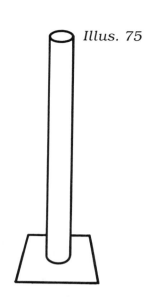

Illus. 75

Now you need a piece of waxed paper and a rubber band. If you don't have waxed paper handy, try using kitchen plastic wrap. Cut a square of waxed paper about 2 inches wider than the distance across the tube.

Place the open end of the cardboard tube in the middle of the waxed paper. Illus. 75 shows how. Pull up the ends of the paper onto the sides of the tube as shown in Illus. 76. Wrap the rubber band around the paper to hold it in place.

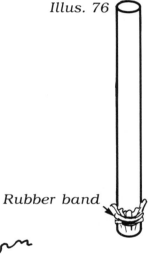

Illus. 76

Poke five or six holes through the side of the tube about 2 inches from the end. Be careful when making these holes. You don't want holes in your finger and you don't want to bend or collapse the tube.

Once the holes are made, place the open end over your mouth as in Illus. 77. Hum a little tune into the tube.

The vibration of the waxed paper should create a different humming sound—not really musical, but different.

Rubber band

Experiment to create the best sound. Hum loudly and softly. Try a longer or a shorter tube. A fat tube allows you to get your mouth and nose both covered to create a really fine hum.

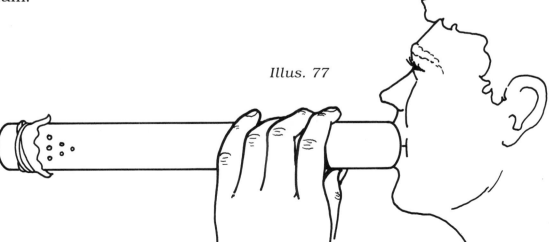

Illus. 77

· 3 ·
Balance, Tumble, and Jump

Easy Balance

To make your first Easy Balance, begin with a piece from a cereal box about 7 inches long and 4 inches wide. Cut a piece of notebook paper the same size and fold it double so that it looks like Illus. 78.

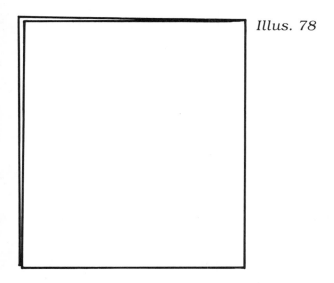

Illus. 78

Illus. 79

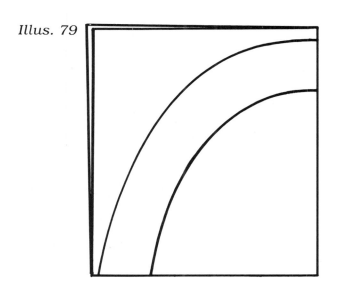

Draw an outline on the paper to match Illus. 79. With the paper still folded, cut out the drawing. Trace this pattern onto the cereal box; then cut out the figure.

When the figure is cut out, tape a bit of weight onto each arm, as in Illus. 80. Small metal washers or pennies are great weights.

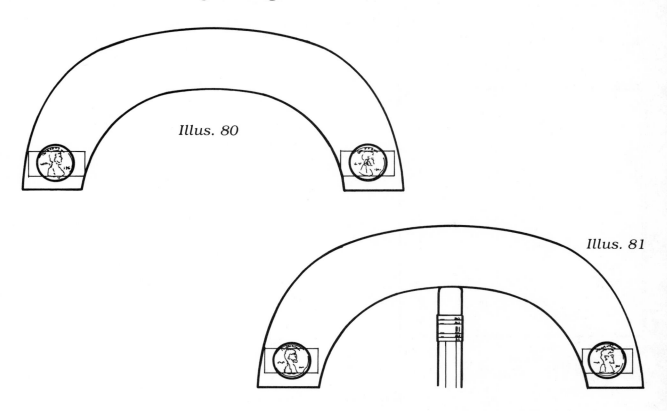

Illus. 80

Illus. 81

Balance the weighted toy on the end of your finger for a test; then move on to the end of a pencil as in Illus. 81. If you blow very gently on one arm of the toy, it will spin slowly around and around on the eraser without falling off.

With just a little imagination you can think of a number of places to leave your toy balanced and waiting to be noticed.

Make other Easy Balance toys with longer arms, thinner or fatter bodies, and artistic shapes. For instance, you can think of the arms as the wings on a bird and cut out your next Easy Balance so that it has a bird's head in its center. Draw in some wing feathers and you can leave your Easy Balance Bird perched in any number of amazing places.

Try an Easy Balance with very long arms that reach down, rather than out. Always tape the washers or pennies near the ends of the arms for the best balance. This one will be really hard to throw off.

The Tumbler

The tube from a toilet roll is a good beginning for this little toy which tumbles over and over down a sloping surface.

You need two pieces each, about 4 inches square, and two rubber bands. You also need something heavy and round to go inside the Tumbler. A golf ball or a big marble works best.

Place one end of the tube in the middle of one of the paper squares. Pull up the edges of the paper as in Illus. 82. Wrap a rubber band around the loose edges to keep the paper tightly in place.

Drop the ball or a marble into the tube. Now place the other square of paper on the open end and fold it down into place. Wrap the second rubber band around the top paper and your Tumbler is ready to go, as in Illus. 83.

In order to tumble end over end this toy needs a sloping surface. The surface needs to be a little rough so that the ends of the toy have something to catch on instead of just letting the Tumbler slide.

Test your Tumbler by tipping a sofa cushion up at one end and letting the toy tumble end over end down the cushion. Now go looking for a longer run so that the toy can really show its stuff.

Try drawing a face at one end of the tube and feet at the other; then Tumbler becomes a little figure who rolls head over heels downhill.

Make smaller models with just one regular marble. Make the small tubes out of file cards and a piece of transparent tape instead of a rubber band.

Tumblers make quite a display when they go end over end down a slanted surface, especially if each little Tumbler is colored differently.

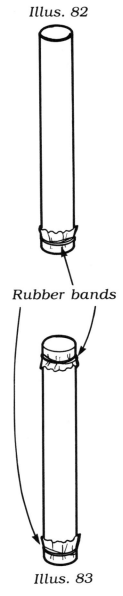

Illus. 82

Rubber bands

Illus. 83

This tumbles real well!

Jumper

The side of a cereal box is perfect for your first Jumper. Draw the outline from Illus. 84 on your piece of cardboard. This will create a square box that measures 1½ inches in all directions. Naturally, you can make a larger or a smaller box by changing the dimensions.

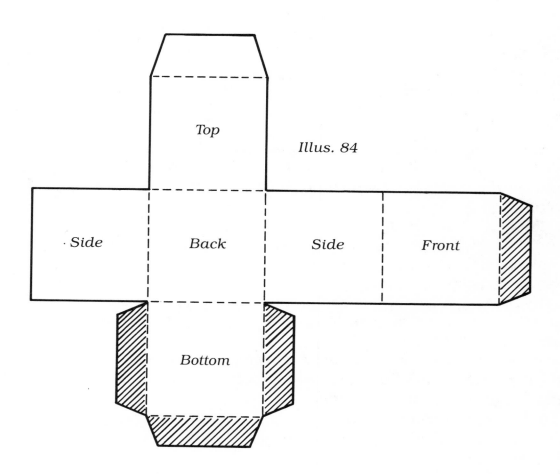

Illus. 84

Four flaps are shaded in the drawing. These flaps will be tucked away inside the box when you assemble it. The fifth flap, the unshaded one, is a tiny bit larger than the other flaps. It will hold the lid shut when the box is complete.

Each dotted line is a fold. To get an absolutely straight fold in the cardboard, score the fold first. Scoring puts a little groove in the material without cutting the cardboard. Hold the edge of the ruler along the fold lines, and hold a table knife (don't use a sharp knife) right down at the tip. Press the tip along the fold line. This makes a little crease in the cardboard which will help make a perfectly straight fold. Score and fold along all the dotted lines.

Lay a ruler or other straightedge along the line to be scored. Hold the table knife right down near the point and press down firmly. Pull the blunt point of the table knife along the line to be scored. It will make a crease or groove in the material. Fold the material along this groove and you will get a nice straight crease. Score and fold along all the dotted lines.

Now the box will just about finish itself. Fold the front, back, and two sides into a square. Put a bit of glue or a piece of transparent tape on the front tab and tuck it under the side. Check to see which side of the tab needs the glue!

Do the same for the three bottom tabs. Be sure that you glue the sides of the tabs which will touch the insides of the box. Check before gluing! Finally, fold the bottom into place with the tabs inside the box.

Illus. 85 shows the finished box. The lid is all set to be folded down to close it.

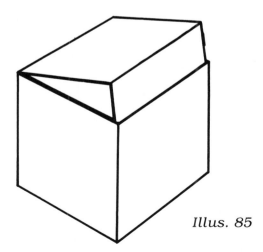

Illus. 85

49

Now take a piece of cereal box cardboard and make a spring for Jumper.

Cut a piece of cardboard about 12 inches long. Make it ¼ inch narrower than the width of your box. To make it into a spring, bend the cardboard without folding it. A good way to do this is to bend each fold around a pencil, as in Illus. 86. Just sort of wrap the material around the pencil and rub the bend into place.

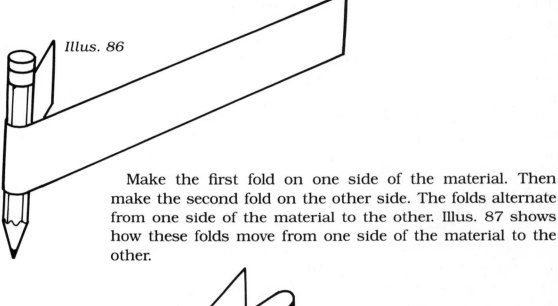

Illus. 86

Make the first fold on one side of the material. Then make the second fold on the other side. The folds alternate from one side of the material to the other. Illus. 87 shows how these folds move from one side of the material to the other.

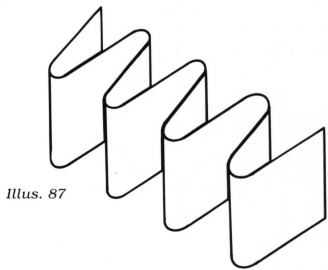

Illus. 87

When the entire strip has the bends or folds in place, stuff it into the box. Press it down into the bottom of the box and make sure that each bend goes in the right direction. Close the lid and wait for someone to open the box.

If the Jumper pushes the lid open, you may need to put something on top of the box to hold it shut. A rubber band around the box does the trick.

To make certain someone opens the box, why not write *DO NOT OPEN* on top of the lid? Who can resist opening it then?

Works every time!!!

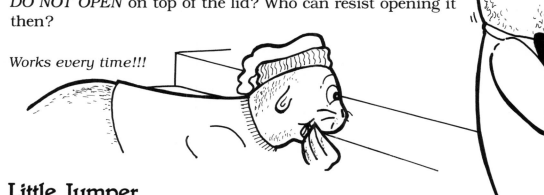

Little Jumper

This little jack-in-the-box uses a match folder. It is easy to make and is good for a laugh.

First, make a cat spring. Cut two strips of notebook or typing paper about ½ inch wide and as long as the paper.

Staple, tape, or glue the strips together so that they are at right angles, as in Illus. 88.

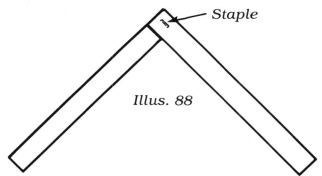

— Staple

Illus. 88

Now fold the bottom strip over the top strip and crease the fold into place. Next, fold the other strip over and crease it. Illus. 89 shows how this works.

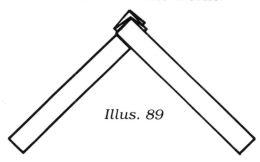

Illus. 89

Keep repeating this until there is no more paper left to fold over.

Fasten the final fold with a bit of transparent tape or glue, and your cat spring is finished.

Get an *empty* match folder from your mom or dad and open it. Glue or tape the bottom of the spring onto the rear cover. Illus. 90 shows how. Slip the cover closed and wait for someone to open the folder looking for matches.

Illus. 90

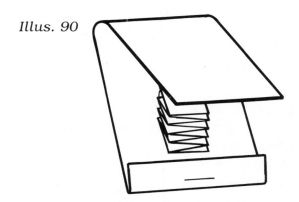

Of course, you can make several cat springs and glue them into one long spring. This gives more spring to Little Jumper when the cover is opened.

String Walker

A sheet of cereal box material and five plastic drinking straws will become a String Walker with a little bit of work.

Cut a strip of cereal box about 2 inches wide and 9 inches long. Score it along the dotted lines in Illus. 91.

Illus. 91

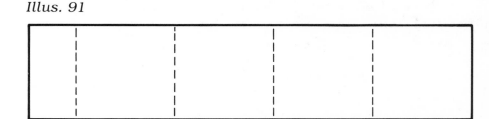

Fold the strip into a hollow square. Glue or tape the flap down so that the box does not unfold. Illus. 92 shows the hollow square.

Next, cut a strip of cardboard 2 inches wide and 7 inches long. Score it along the dotted lines in Illus. 93.

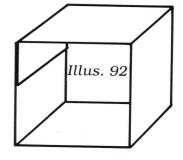

Illus. 92

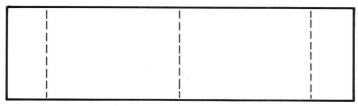

Illus. 93

Now fold it along the scored lines so that it forms a top for the square. Tape or glue this piece so that it matches Illus. 94.

Cut two pieces of cardboard, each 1 × 1½ inches. Score them along the dotted lines in Illus. 95. Now fold each of the pieces along the scored line. Set these aside for just a minute.

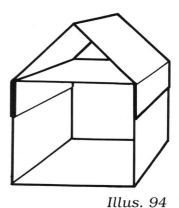

Illus. 94

Illus. 95

Now take one straw and cut it into two equal pieces. Use your scissors to cut in from each end as shown in Illus. 96. It is important that these cuts be exactly opposite each other. Make sure that one cut is ½ inch from one end of the straw and the other is ¾ inch.

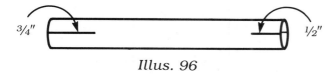

Illus. 96

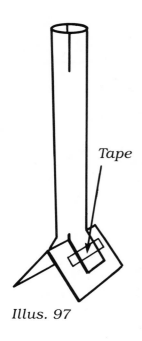

Slip one of these small pieces of cardboard into the ½-inch slit in one of the straws. Illus. 97 shows this step. Use two strips of tape to hold the straw firmly to the cardboard, so that String Walker has a foot. Do the same for the second straw.

Poke two holes in String Walker's base, just big enough for the plastic straws to go through. Put the holes where you see them in Illus. 98. Be careful and don't poke your finger.

Tape

Illus. 97

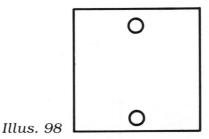

Illus. 98

Slip one straw through one hole. Spread the ¾-inch cut at the end of the straw. Use a piece of tape to fasten the spread ends firmly onto the base. Be sure that the foot points straight ahead.

Fasten the second straw into place in the same way. Illus. 99 shows your progress thus far.

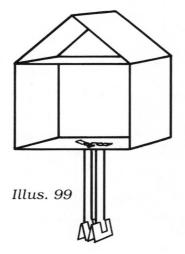

Illus. 99

Now to make String Walker's arms. They need to be nice and long for good balance. Cut a 1-inch slit in one end of one straw, as in Illus. 100. This time, only cut one side of the straw.

Illus. 100

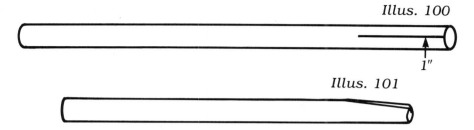

1″

Illus. 101

Push one side of the cut under the other side, to form a point as in Illus. 101. Slip this point into the end of the second straw and push the two straws firmly together. Use a strip of tape to fasten the two together as in Illus. 102. Do the same with the other two plastic straws and both arms are finished.

Illus. 102

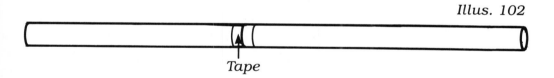

Tape

Tape one end of each arm firmly onto the top of String Walker. Illus. 103 shows how.

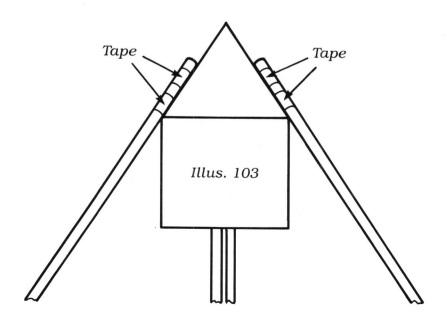

Tape   *Tape*

Illus. 103

Cut a piece of string or thread about 2 feet long. Find a metal washer or two and thread the string through them.

Tape both ends of the string or thread to the ends of the Walker's arms, as in Illus. 104.

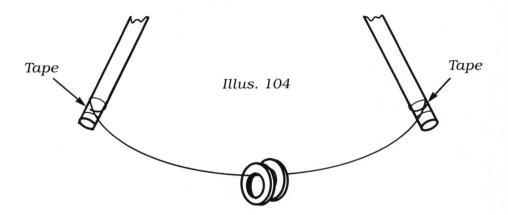

Tape   *Illus. 104*   *Tape*

String Walker is ready to perform.

Tie one end of a string to a cupboard handle, the back of a chair, or any other firm anchor. Hold the other end in your hand or tie it to another firm spot.

Place String Walker's feet on the string. Make sure the washer or other weight is hanging directly below its feet. Let go! Your Walker should balance on the string.

Test its balance by tipping it a bit to one side or the other. It should sway back and forth but not lose its balance. If it does lose its balance, it probably needs a bit more weight added to the washers.

Be sure the balancing string is tight. A loose, sagging string will make String Walker fall.

Jiggle the string and Walker will move forward or backwards. This works best when you hold one end of the string while the other is tied up.

Try making some String Walkers smaller or larger. Just remember that with all balancing toys the longer the arms are, the better they keep their balance.

String Dancer

Begin this project by drawing the arms, legs, and body of your String Dancer on a piece of cereal box material. These body parts do not need to look exactly like a human body. In fact, the body itself can end up looking a bit like a potato and your String Dancer won't mind in the least. Illus. 105 gives you an idea of how to make these body parts.

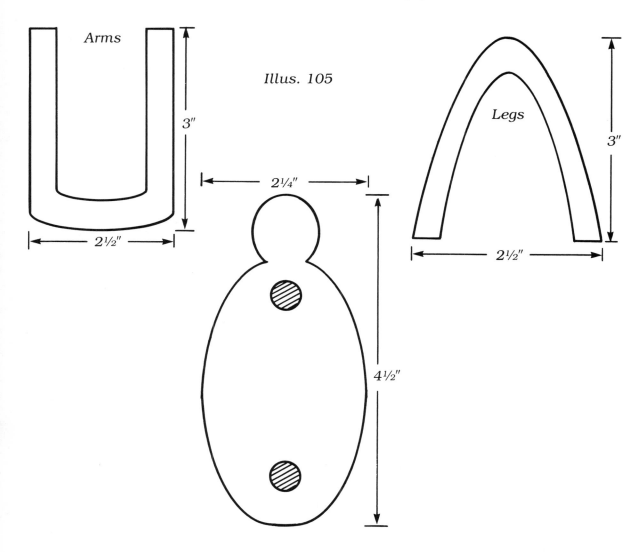

Illus. 105

Carefully cut out the two shaded circles in the body. Make them about ⅝ inch across. If you find the arms and legs won't turn inside the circles, you can make them a bit bigger, but don't make the leg circle too large. If it is, the Dancer's legs may come off while it is performing.

Slip the arms and legs into the hole in the body. If either the arms or legs are too tight, remove them and make the hole a little larger. Put this aside for a little while.

Cut two pieces of light cardboard, about 4 × 5 inches. Fold each of them three times along the dotted lines in Illus. 106. Use a couple of pieces of tape to keep the folded material together so that it does not unfold in your hands.

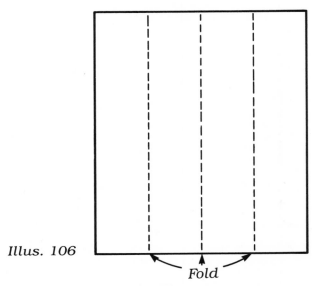

Illus. 106

Fold

Now make some small holes in this material and on Dancer's hands. An awl or the sharp point of a scissors will do the job. Make the holes in the cardboard and the arms as in Illus. 107.

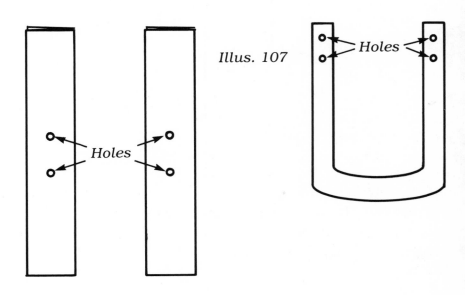

Illus. 107

Holes

Holes

58

Now comes the time to string your String Dancer. Do this part carefully, because one mistake will mean you'll have to start all over again.

Take a piece of string or thread about 3 feet long. Thread is best because you can use a needle to guide it through the holes in the cardboard. If you use thread, use it double-thick to make it stronger.

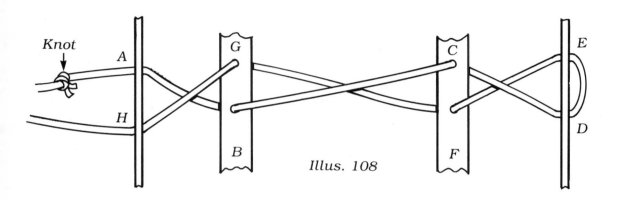

Illus. 108

Follow these directions one step at a time, and keep checking Illus. 108.

Place the two chunks of folded cardboard on either side of Dancer's hands as in Illus. 108. Be sure that Dancer's arms are already through its body at this point. Otherwise, you will have a pair of dancing arms and no body!

Thread the string through hole A. Tie a big knot in the end so that the thread of string won't pull through the hole as you continue to work.

Now go through hole B. Come in from the back of the material as seen in Illus. 108.

Go through the front of hole C.

Thread through hole D.

Thread through hole E.

Now cross the string already in place and go through hole F. Make certain that you go through hole F from the front.

Go behind the string on your way to hole G. Go through hole G from the back.

Cross the string already in place and thread it through hole H.

Carefully pull the string tight. Work the slack out of it so that there is about 1 inch of space between each hand and the cardboard piece.

Finally, tie the loose ends firmly together.

To make String Dancer dance, hold the two cardboard pieces in your hands. Pull them apart a bit. The string will begin to untwist and give the Dancer a rocking motion.

Let your hands come together just a bit and Dancer will rock in the opposite direction. Pull them apart and Dancer will rock in the opposite direction and turn a flip in the air. By pulling and releasing the pressure, you will spin String Dancer forward and backwards. With a bit of practice you can make it stand on its head, stop halfway through a spin, and do a variety of stunts. If you keep the string untangled, Dancer will perform for a long time.

Make a face for Dancer and color clothing for its body. Try making smaller or larger versions of String Dancer. It is up to you and your imagination.

String Roller

This funny little fellow rolls back and forth along the string.

Let's make the roller first. A cardboard tube such as the tube out of a roll of toilet tissue is a must. Cut a ring off the end of the tube as in Illus. 109, about ⅜ inch wide. Carefully push the end of your scissors through the tube to keep the ring whole.

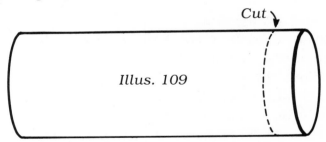

Cut

Illus. 109

Cut two circles out of cereal box cardboard. These circles should be 1 inch larger than the ring you just cut from the cardboard tube. Draw them with a compass or a jar lid to be neat. Poke a small hole through the middle of each circle. Try to make it the very center.

It is time to assemble the wheel. In Illus. 110 you see two little pieces of transparent tape stuck to the inside of the ring. Place one of the cardboard circles on top of the ring. The tape will hold the two together.

Turn the wheel over and do the same thing with the second cardboard circle. Be sure that the central holes are exactly opposite each other and the ring is right in the center of the cardboard circles, and your wheel will look like Illus. 111.

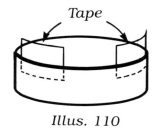

Illus. 110

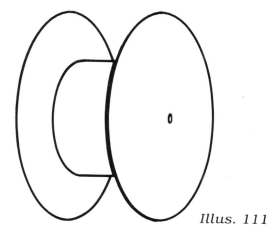

Illus. 111

To make the wheel good and strong and to keep the string from slipping between the ring and the cardboard circles, you need to do a bit of glue work. Run the glue all the way around the point where each circle meets the central ring; then put the wheel aside for a little while.

From cereal box cardboard cut out the tall, thin fellow seen in Illus. 112. He's about 2 inches wide and 12 inches long. If your cardboard is not quite 12 inches long, just make him as long as your material.

It is time to go back to the wheel. Make certain that the glue is dry; then get a round toothpick or piece of wire for the wheel's axle.

Push the axle through the holes in the middle of the cardboard circles. Make sure there is as much axle sticking out from one side as from the other.

Illus. 112

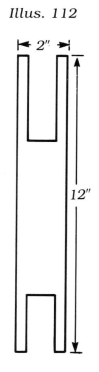

Cut off two pieces of plastic drinking straw, about ½ inch long. Slip these pieces over the ends of the axle, so that they look like Illus. 113.

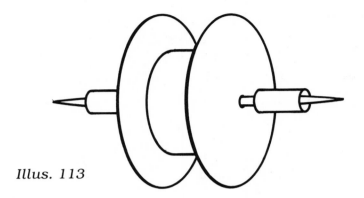

Illus. 113

Cut two pieces of cereal box, each about ½ inch square. Push the ends of the axle through each piece, and put a drop of glue on the axle end as in Illus. 114. This will keep the axle and wheel together.

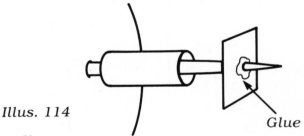

Illus. 114

Glue

Sometimes the spool loses its cool!

Use a short piece of tape to fasten the Roller's hands to the plastic straw pieces as in Illus. 115.

Make sure that the wheel turns easily. If the Roller's hands press against the wheel, trim a bit of material off the sides of its hands.

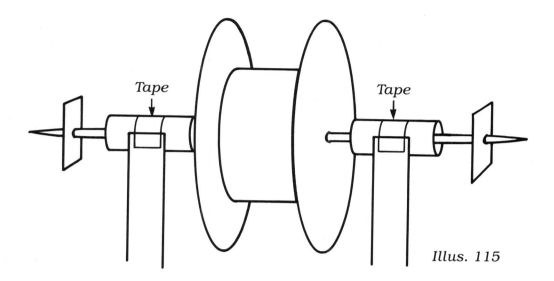

Illus. 115

Tie one end of a fairly long string to a cupboard door, chair, or any other solid object. Slip the wheel over the string. Now run the string downhill and tie the other end to something else solid. Let the Roller go, and it should ride right down the string.

If you don't want to go to all the work of pushing it back to the high end of the string for its next ride, instead of tying the second end of the string to a chair or some other object, hold it in your hand. When your hand is lower than the other end of the string, the Roller will come to you. Raise your hand and it will go in reverse, back to the starting point.

· 4 ·
Puppets

Finger Puppets

Finger Puppets are great for entertaining little children and are easy to make.

Take a 3 × 4-inch piece of typing or notebook paper and roll it into a hollow tube to fit over your finger. A piece of transparent tape along the seam will make sure that the tube does not unroll. Illus. 116 shows this tube.

Cut a strip of paper about ¾ inch wide and 5 or 6 inches long. This will become your Finger Puppet's hands and arms.

Tape this strip to the rear of the tube as in Illus. 117. Tuck the end of the tape into the open end of the tube at the bottom to make sure that your puppet's arms don't come loose.

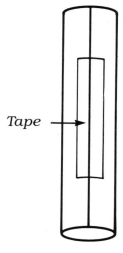

Tape

Illus. 116

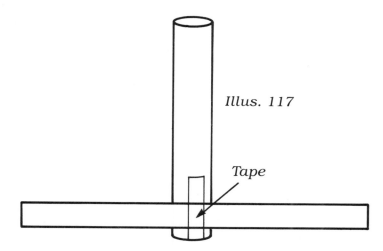

Illus. 117

Tape

Bend the two hands around the front of the tube and put the ends together. With your scissors, cut thumbs and fists for your puppet, or a thumb and four fingers, if you want. Check Illus. 118 to see one way your puppet's hands can look.

Illus. 118

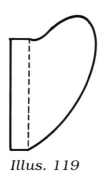

Illus. 119

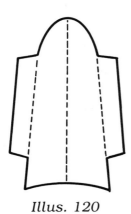

Illus. 120

Do you want ears for your Finger Puppet? Fold a piece of paper and draw the pattern in Illus. 114. Once the ears are cut out, fold them along the dotted line so that the flap is at right angles to the ear. Use just a drop of glue on this flap to glue the ear to the side of the tube.

Illus. 120 shows the pattern for the puppet's nose. Once you have this cut out, fold it along the central dotted line; then fold back both flaps along the dotted lines. Glue the backs of the flaps and press the nose into place on the puppet's face.

Illus. 121 shows your Finger Puppet with its arms, ears, and nose in place.

Draw on eyes and a mouth for your puppet, and maybe even sleeves of a coat along its arms. Color its hair or even give it a moustache. For a hat, color a strip of paper and wrap it around the puppet's head and tape or glue it into place.

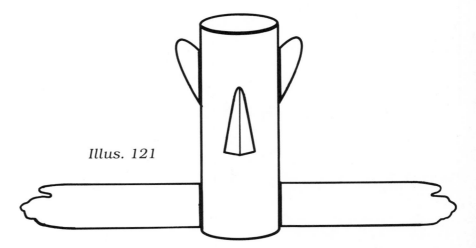

Illus. 121

Slip your Finger Puppet over your middle finger so that the nose faces away from you. Use your forefinger and ring finger to make its arms move together and apart.

Put a Finger Puppet on each hand and have them talk to each other.

Make shorter or taller Finger Puppets than this one. They can be fatter or a little thinner. Tubes from paper-towel rolls make fine Finger Puppets.

If you want a really plump puppet, use the tube from a roll of toilet tissue. You may need to put two fingers inside it to keep it from slipping off your hand.

Arm Wavers

Cut a piece of cereal box or manila folder about 8 × 10 inches. Draw a body outline like the one in Illus. 122. This puppet will be a Humpty Dumpty sort of fellow. This outline is only an idea. Use your imagination and come up with a better design. Cut out the body and set it to one side for a few minutes.

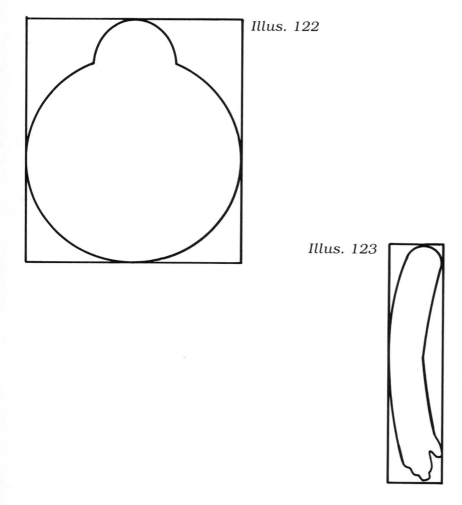

Illus. 122

Illus. 123

Illus. 123 shows an outline for the puppet's arms. Make a pattern on notebook paper; then draw two arms exactly alike on the cardboard or manila material. Two pieces of material 2 inches wide and 8 inches long will do nicely for the arms.

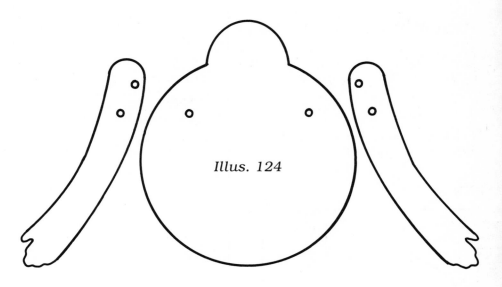

Illus. 124

It is now hole-poking time. Remember to be careful and make two holes in each arm as shown in Illus. 124. Make the two holes in the body as well. These holes should be just large enough to let the end of a piece of string or a paper fastener (the little brass fellow in Illus. 125) through them.

Illus. 125

It is now assembly time. Push the paper fastener through the holes in the puppet's body so that the points come out the back. Slip the arms over the pointed ends as in Illus. 126. Spread the pointed ends and your puppet is half done.

Illus. 126

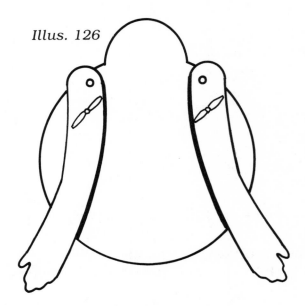

If you don't have two paper fasteners, use two paper clips. Bend them so that they look like Illus. 127. Push the single wire through the body so that the unbent part of the clip is on the front of the puppet. Now slip the puppet arm onto the single end of the clip. Once the arm is in place, bend the clip over flat against the arm and put a piece of tape over the end of the clip. This is shown in Illus. 128.

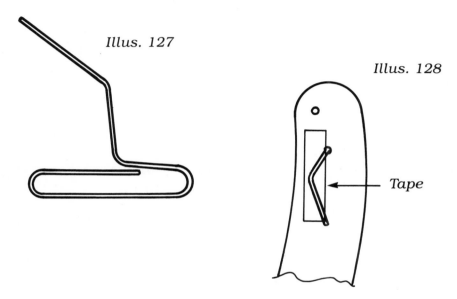

Illus. 127

Illus. 128

Tape

After both arms are attached, cut a piece of string about 10 inches long. Thread it through the top holes in the puppet arms and tie both ends firmly. Illus. 129 shows this step.

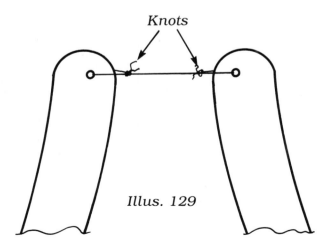

Knots

Illus. 129

Cut a second piece of string about 1½ feet in length. Tie it to the middle of the first string as in Illus. 130.

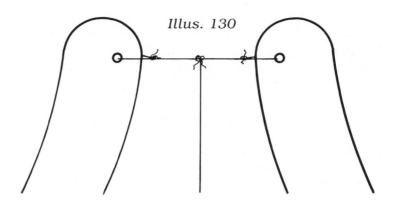

Illus. 130

Hold the puppet's body firmly in one hand. Grasp the loose end of the string in the other. To make your puppet wave its arms, just pull down on the string.

Give this roly-poly little puppet some eyes, a mouth, and a nose. Color on some ears as well. A broad belt right around its middle might be a good idea.

Give its arms some extra interest and draw on a wrist-watch or a bracelet or two. For that matter, you can even color on some shirt sleeves and then color the rest of the shirt onto the body.

Heh, heh, heh!

Think about some other ideas for Arm Wavers. They don't have to wave just their arms. How about a rabbit who waves its ears? What about a girl with her hair in braids that stand out to one side? Maybe a pointy-headed clown whose long ears rise and fall at the side of his head?

Illus. 131 shows a few of these ideas.

When you try some of these other ideas you will need to place the ears or hair a little differently than you did the arms for your first Arm Waver.

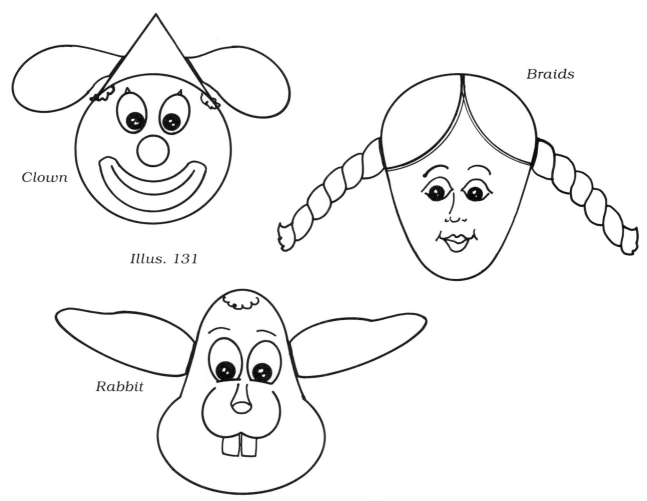

Clown

Braids

Illus. 131

Rabbit

Think about how you want to color or design your puppet's face or body before you attach the arms. It is lots easier to draw or color features on the material while it is flat, without the fasteners and arms in place.

If you have young children in your family or neighborhood, these puppets will give them lots of laughs.

Wave and Kick Puppets

These puppets are just like the Arm Wavers, but have not only arms but legs as well. Cereal box material is fine for these puppets. So is any stiff cardboard which is fairly light in weight.

Color your Wave and Kick Puppets before cutting them out. This is usually easier than after they're assembled. Don't try to get too fancy with these puppets. Keep the arms and legs fairly simple.

Let's do a roly-poly clown for our first Wave and Kick Puppet. Clowns are fun because no costume design is too far out for a clown. Let your imagination take your crayons where it will.

Illus. 132 shows one way you might design your clown's arms, legs, and body, but don't worry if your clown turns up looking different from the one in the illustration. The circles in the arms and legs that are shown by the little arrows are the circles you will tie the control strings into. Use paper fasteners or paper clips for the others. Check page 71 if you need help with the paper clips.

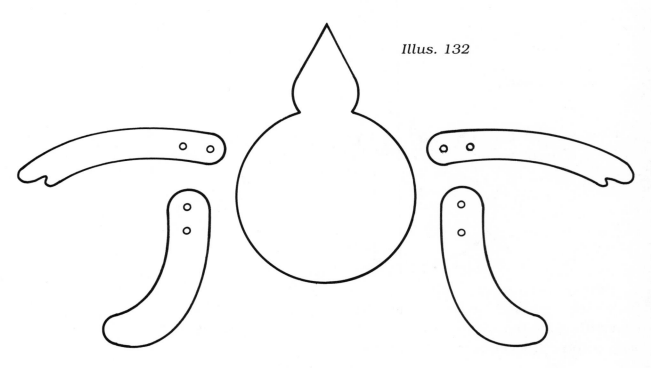

Illus. 132

When you have the pieces colored and cut out and all the holes punched, put your Wave and Kick Puppet together. Illus. 133 shows the rear view of the assembled puppet.

Make all the knots good and tight, and be sure when you tie the control string from the legs onto the long control string which operates the puppet that you make the knot so that it won't slip.

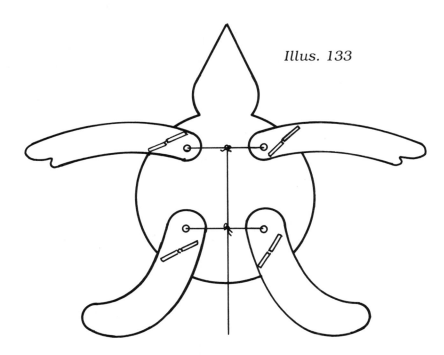

Illus. 133

A good way to do this is to first tie the leg control string onto the main string. Tie just half a knot in the leg string; then gently check for distance by pulling the long string to see how the arms and legs work. Be sure to leave a long loose end on the main string so that it will reach to the arm control and still leave room for the knot.

Once you are sure the legs are working properly, wrap the long string around the control string for the legs two or three turns. Tie a double knot in the long string.

Now wrap the loose end of the main string around the control string for the arms. Tie it in a single knot and check to make sure that the arms and legs work together. If they don't, retie the string with less distance between the arm and leg knots on the main string. When you get things working, tie the last knot tightly.

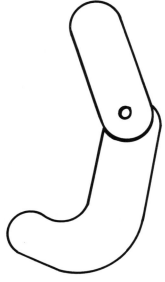

Illus. 134

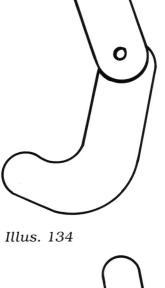

Once you have made one of these puppets, it is easy to make others. Any animal, such as a bear, makes a good Wave and Kick Puppet. Just keep the arms and legs simple and do a nice job of coloring. You could also make one that is just a person's head. A man with a huge moustache and hair (hooked up just like the legs and arms) would be a lot of fun.

The head and shoulders of an animal or person are another possibility. A rabbit's ears and front paws can work together. If you really want to get fancy, try a rabbit whose ears and front and back paws all work together. Then you have three parts instead of two to attach to the main control string. Robots, monsters, and aliens are also good ideas.

Once you are expert at making these puppets, here is another idea. Illus. 134 shows how to make joints at the elbows and knees of your puppet. Paper fasteners are best if you have them. If not, use the bent paper clip idea, and remember to tape the loose end of the clip onto the back of the arm or leg so that it does not slip out of place.

Springy

Construction paper works best for Springy. Notebook or typing paper is fine, too.

Springy is made out of cat springs, which give it its bounce. The first step is to make five of these folded cat springs. Take two strips of paper about 2½ inches wide and 24 to 30 inches long. To get paper that long, just cut half a dozen strips of paper, each 2½ inches wide, and tape, glue, or staple two or three of them into one long strip.

I knew I'd get him back!

76

If you are using construction paper, try making one strip of paper from one color and the other strip out of another color. If you want a colorful clown, use three or four colors when you put the long strips of paper together. This will give your puppet a really different body.

To make a cat spring, fasten one end of a long strip to the other end at right angles, as in Illus. 135. Now fold one piece over the other and crease the fold. This step is shown in Illus. 136.

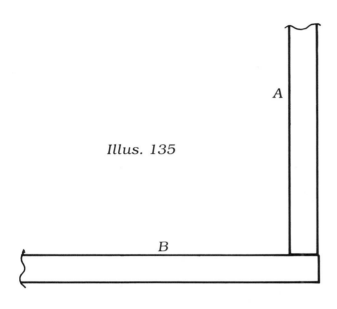

Illus. 135

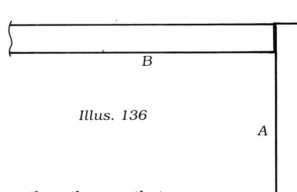

Illus. 136

Keep folding one strip of paper over the other so that your cat spring gets thicker and thicker. When there is no paper left to fold, glue or tape the top together so that the spring won't unfold, and your body is finished.

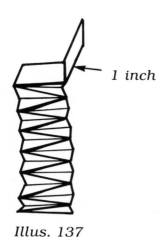

1 inch

Illus. 137

Now for the arms and legs. Each arm and leg requires two strips of paper 1 inch wide and 20 to 24 inches long. Make cat springs for the arms and legs just as you did for the body, with one difference. Leave about 1 inch as in Illus. 137 at the end of the spring. Do not fold it.

Glue or tape the cat spring together so that the final inch of paper is left sticking up. This will let you fasten the arm or leg to the body.

When all four arms and legs are finished, it is time to start putting Springy together. Illus. 138 shows how to glue or tape the ends of the arms onto the top of the body. Once the arms are firmly fastened into place, turn the puppet over and attach the legs in the same manner.

Illus. 138   Tape or glue

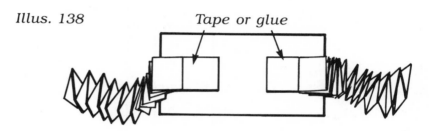

What's a puppet without a head? Since this is a clown, let's give our Springy puppet a round head with wild hair. Illus. 139 shows how to make the puppet's head with a long neck so that we can attach it to the body. The dotted line in Illus. 139 indicates where to fold the long neck. Glue or tape the bottom of the neck onto the top of the body.

Illus. 139

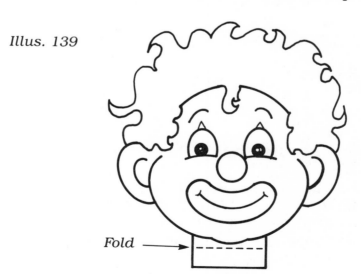

Fold →

78

Hands and feet are no problem. They can be as simple or as complicated as you want. Illus. 140 shows simple ideas for hands and feet. Once you cut out the hands and feet, glue or tape them directly to the ends of the arms and legs.

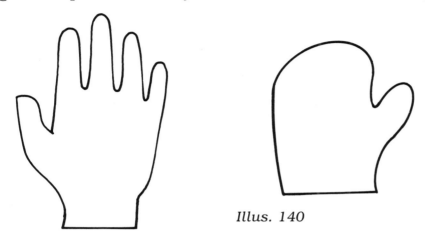
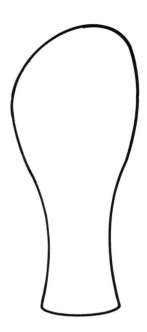

Illus. 140

Now you need a piece of string about 3 feet long to control Springy. Either poke a hole in each hand or tape the ends of the string to the hands.

When the string is pulled, your puppet will move. The harder you pull the string, the more your puppet will dance and spring about. Illus. 141 shows the hands with the string attached.

Illus. 141

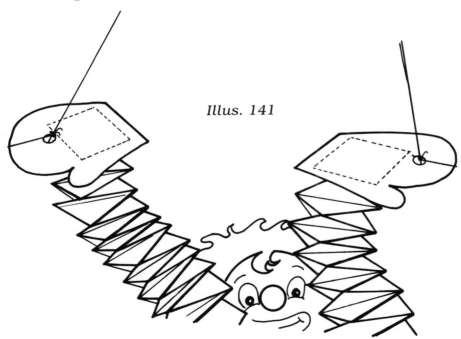

If you want to be really fancy (and why not?), cut the control string in the middle. Roll a tube of paper for a control stick and tape the roll in two or three places so that it won't unroll. Tie one control string to each end of the tube as in Illus. 142.

Illus. 142

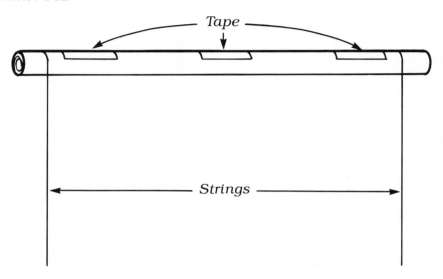

If you pull straight up on your control tube, the puppet will move straight up. However, if you lift one end of the tube, then the other, you can make your puppet lift one leg, then the other.

Try lifting up one end of the control tube and moving it slightly forward. This will lift a leg and move it forward. Practise a few minutes and your Springy puppet will have a bouncy little walk.

Don't forget how to use the control tube. You will use it again.

Hand Puppet

The Hand Puppet is easy to make and fun to use. This one is especially good if you want to entertain younger children. Its arms move, its hands clap, and you don't even have to make hands and arms. Its hands and arms are your fingers and thumbs.

The first step is to make its body to fit your own hand. Use a sheet of typing paper, notebook paper, or construction paper. Place your hand flat on the paper as in Illus. 143 with your three middle fingers together and your little finger and thumb stretched out a bit. With your pencil make a dot or a small line beside the index finger and the ring finger. The arrows show where to make these marks. The width of your three fingers tells you exactly how large to make the Hand Puppet's body.

Illus. 143

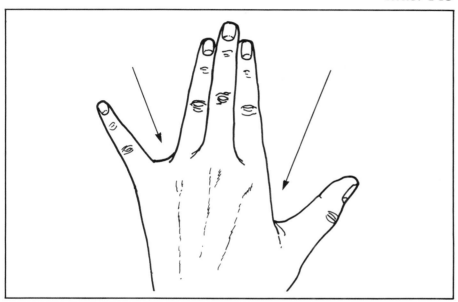

I guess fingers would help!

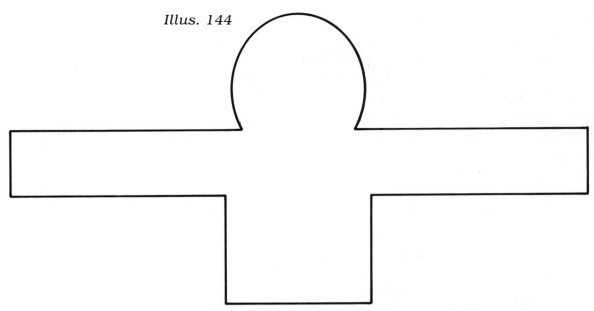

Take your hand away and draw the puppet's body out-line. Keep the body simple and make it large enough to cover your hand and wrist. Keep in mind that it must be narrow enough at one spot so that your thumb and little finger can reach around and become the puppet's arms. Illus. 144 shows a basic body design. The long flaps at either side of the body are not part of the puppet's body. They will fasten the puppet to your hand. Illus. 145 shows how. Once you have them measured so that you know they fit your hand, glue or tape these flaps together. Slip your fingers over the flap and your puppet is ready for action.

Illus. 145

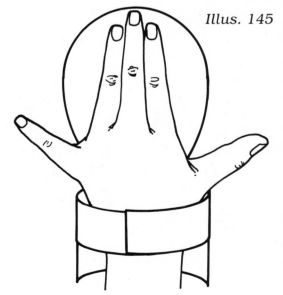

Take just a second and check to be sure your thumb and little finger can move freely. If not, trim a little off the sides of the body. You don't want to have a puppet whose arms can only stick straight out.

Now to give your Hand Puppet some character. Color the body or glue on clothing. You can color part of the puppet and glue on a few things, such as hats, long hair, a big nose, or even a beard.

A male puppet might look good with a tie and belt. A female puppet may prefer a dress or nice blouse. Illus. 146 will give you a few ideas for dressing your Hand Puppets. You may already have some ideas of your own.

There is no wrong way to dress this puppet or any other puppet you make. Each puppet is your own creation. Feel free to color it or add to it in any way you wish. That's the fun of these little fellows.

Illus. 146

In Illus. 146 the male's hat, nose, beard, tie, and belt have been all cut out of colored paper and pasted on. His eyes are drawn on with a crayon. The female puppet's hair and dress were cut out of colored paper and glued onto the puppet. Her features were colored on with crayon.

To make the puppet perform, slip your hand into the flap. Use your thumb and little finger as arms. If you want your puppet's head to nod, just bend your other fingers forward.

Make one for each hand and the two can put on their own little show. It is very easy to work both hands at the same time.

Tube Puppet

Many people call this type of puppet a marionette. It has joints and can walk, wave, and make all sorts of lifelike movements. In order to do this, it has five control strings and the operator has to use both hands and spend some time practising to make the puppet do its best.

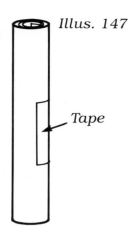

Illus. 147

Tape

Illus. 148

Illus. 149

Make your first Tube Puppet's arms and legs from rolled paper tubes. If you want to use plastic drinking straws for a later model, that's just fine. Take 8 strips of typing or notebook paper, each about 2 inches wide and as long as the sheet of paper. Roll these strips into eight hollow tubes whose middles are ¼ inch or so across. Don't worry if some tubes end up bigger than others. Use the larger ones for the puppet's legs and all will be well.

Fasten each tube with a strip of tape or a bit of glue so that it does not unroll. Each tube looks like Illus. 147.

Now make two hands and two feet. A piece of the side of a cereal box is just perfect. Make your hands and feet so that they look something like Illus. 148 and Illus. 149.

Now for the body. If you have the tube from a roll of toilet tissue, that is ideal. If not, just make a rolled-paper body. Cut a sheet of notebook paper in half the long way. Tape or glue the two pieces end to end so that you have a strip of paper about 4 inches wide and nearly 2 feet long. Roll this into a hollow tube which is about 1 inch across. Tape it two or three times along the loose edge and your body is ready.

Your puppet's head is another roll of paper. Cut 2 or 3 strips of notebook paper about 1½ inches wide and as long as the sheet of paper. Glue or tape them into one long strip; then roll that strip into a hollow tube. A bit of tape along the outside edge will keep it from unrolling.

Now let's put the Tube Puppet together. Start with its legs. Cut a piece of string about 1½ feet long. Tie a big knot in one end.

Poke a little hole in the middle of one of the puppets and thread the string through it. Push the string through two of the leg tubes, as in Illus. 150.

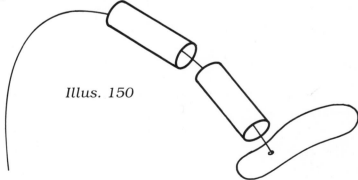

Illus. 150

Here's a hint if you have trouble getting the string through the hollow tubes. Make a needle out of a paper clip or a little piece of wire like the one in Illus. 151. Loop the string through the hook at the end and your problem should be solved.

Poke holes on either side of the body tube. These are the arrows in Illus. 152. Thread the string through these two holes. Now add two more leg tubes and the other foot.

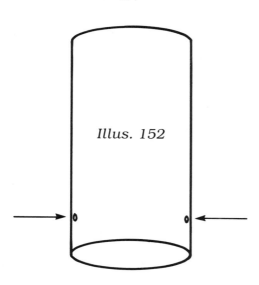

Illus. 152

Illus. 151

Pull the string through the legs and body but do not make it terribly tight. Your puppet's hips and knees have to be able to bend. Tie a big knot under the second foot and trim off any leftover string. Your puppet is shown in Illus. 153.

Assemble the arms exactly the same way that you did the legs.

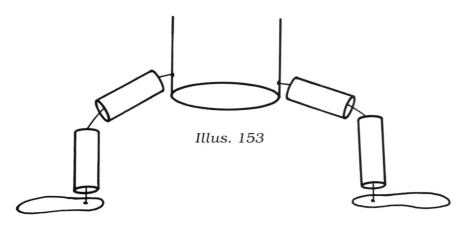

Illus. 153

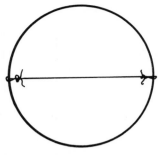

Now for the puppet's head. Make two holes on opposite sides of the body tube. Tie a short piece of string to each hole. The end view of the body tube is in Illus. 154.

Cut a piece of string 1½ feet or so in length. Tie one end to the string you just attached to the body tube. Thread it through the middle of the puppet's head, as in Illus. 155.

Illus. 155

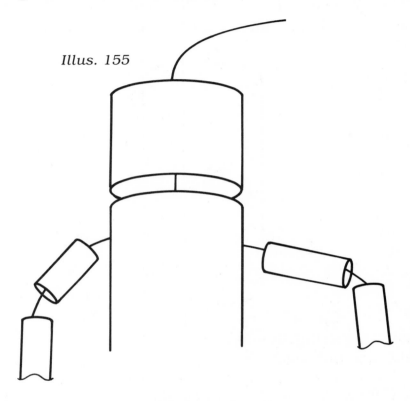

It is time to make your puppet move. You need two control tubes of rolled notebook paper. Make one tube about 8 inches long and the other about 5 inches in length. Naturally, you will tape the loose edges.

Begin with the longer of the two control tubes. Tie the string from the puppet's head firmly in the middle of the control tube. When you lift up on the tube, your puppet should lift up as well.

Now cut two pieces of string about 2 feet long. Tie one end of each string to an end of the control tube. Tie the other end to the bottom end of the top leg piece as in Illus. 156. Poke a hole in the top of the hollow tube and tie the string's end through that hole. You can also tie the end of the string around the tube.

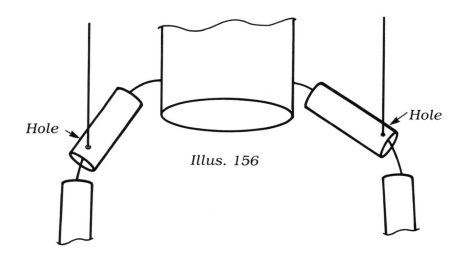

Hole

Hole

Illus. 156

Before you tie these leg control strings to the control tube, measure them carefully so that they are the proper length. When you are holding the control tube up high enough so that the puppet stands straight up, the leg strings need to be perfectly straight up and down. If they are too long, you will have trouble making your puppet's legs move. Illus. 157 shows these strings in place.

Illus. 157

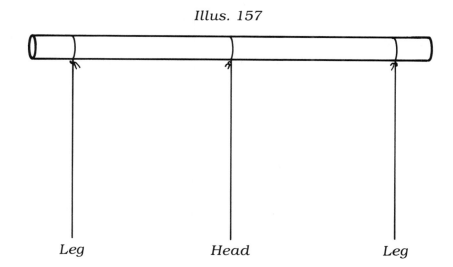

Leg   Head   Leg

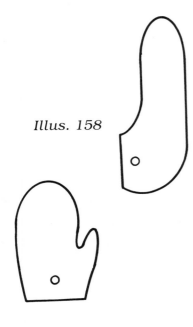

Illus. 158

Be sure to tie each string carefully to an end of the control tube. Tip one end of the control tube, then the other. The puppet will lift one leg, then the other. By turning the tube's ends backwards and forward your puppet's legs will move the same way.

If you need to adjust the length of the leg control strings, it's a simple matter. Just retie the end of the string which goes to the control tube. Make the string longer or shorter.

Cut another two pieces of string, each 1½ feet long. Attach one end of each string to the puppet's wrist in the same way that you just fastened the strings to the puppet's knees. Tie the other end of each arm control string to one end of the short control tube. At this point, your puppet is ready to learn to walk and move.

Practise getting both of your hands to work together. One moves the puppet's legs while the other moves its arms. By lifting and turning the control tubes, Tube Puppet can go for a walk, take a bow, stand up, sit down, and do just about anything you want it to do.

For a second Tube Puppet, try having the hands and feet hang down. To do this, make holes in the hands and feet as in Illus. 158. Tie the string into these holes and assemble the arms and legs just as you did before.

Give your puppet hips and shoulders by making two more rolled paper tubes, each about 2 inches long. Instead of poking holes through the sides of the body tube, run the string through these rolled shoulders and hips. Fasten them to the body tube with tape, as in Illus. 159.

If you decide to use the hip and shoulder method for your puppet, you will attach the puppet's head a little differently than before. Make sure the shoulders are taped firmly to the body.

Tie one end of the head string around the middle of the shoulder piece. Thread the string through the head and up to the control tube as before.

You also can use plastic straws instead of rolled tubes. For that matter, you can give your puppet longer arms and legs just by making the arm and leg tubes longer.

Give your Tube Puppet color by using colored paper, crayons, and paint.

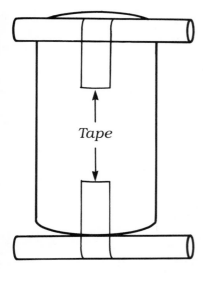

Illus. 159

Tape

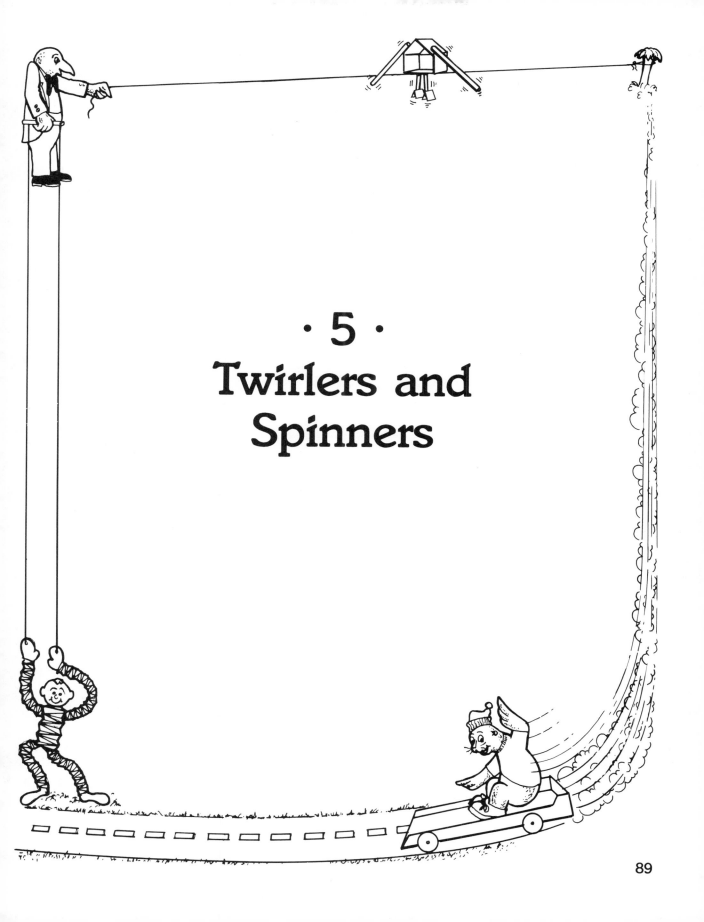

· 5 ·
Twirlers and Spinners

Propeller

Start by making a pattern out of notebook paper. A 5-inch piece is perfect. Fold it double as in Illus. 160. Then draw half the outline on the paper. Be sure to draw along the folded edge.

Cut out the pattern and trace it twice onto a piece of stiff material (a file card is perfect). Cut out the two pieces and tape or glue them at right angles to each other so that your Propeller toy looks like Illus. 161.

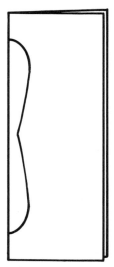

Illus. 160

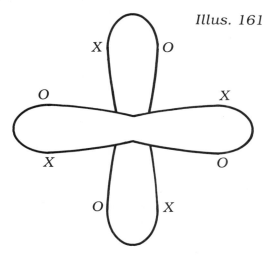

Illus. 161

Now shape your Propeller. Roll and bend the sides of the blades, but do not crease or fold them. Use your thumb and fingers to bend the material.

In Illus. 161 four sides of the blades are marked with "X"s. Roll these sides up. The opposite sides of the blades are marked with little "O"s. Roll these edges down. Don't roll them a great distance. About ¼ inch on each side of the blades is fine.

I don't think you're supposed to ride it!

Now make a mount for your Propeller. Roll a piece of notebook paper into as tight a roll as possible. Try to keep from having any opening at all in the middle. Fasten the loose edge down with a couple of strips of transparent tape. Stick a straight pin through the center of the Propeller and into the end of the rolled mounting. Illus. 162 shows this.

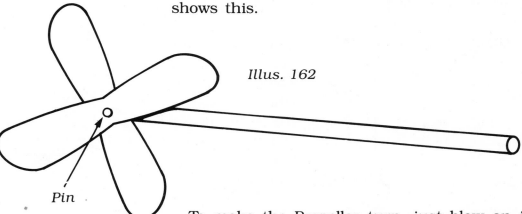

Illus. 162

Pin

To make the Propeller turn, just blow on it. If you are outdoors, hold it in front of you and run with it.

To mount the Propeller, stick the pin through the side of the rolled paper instead of into the end of the roll. It all depends on how you want to hold it. Just don't stick the pin into yourself!

Spinning Star

Cut a sheet of notebook or typing paper in half the long way. Fold one of the half sheets in half the long way. You now have a strip of paper about 2 inches wide and about 1 foot long, as in Illus. 163.

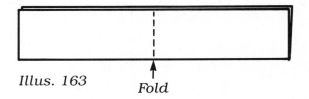

Illus. 163   Fold

Fold one end to the other and crease the fold (the dotted line in Illus. 164.) Open this fold so that the paper is once more a long, narrow strip, two layers thick. This is the center line of the paper strip.

Illus. 164 shows the center fold. The two dotted lines indicate the next folds.

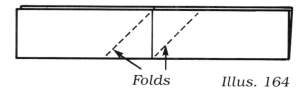

Folds   *Illus. 164*

After you make the next two folds the Star looks like Illus. 165. The dotted lines show the next folds. Make these folds, so that the Star matches Illus. 166. The dotted lines, naturally, show the next folds. But wait! Check Illus. 167 carefully. As you can see, you need to tuck the corner of the fold under the main part of Spinning Star. The dotted lines which run right beside the edge of the main part of the Star are your final folds. Make these two folds and tuck them under the main section. Your Star now looks like Illus. 168. Put this section aside for a little while.

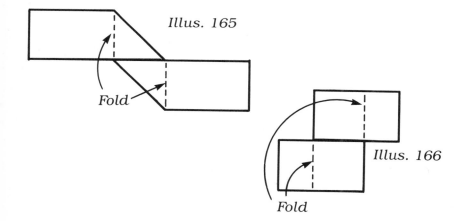

Illus. 165

Fold

Illus. 166

Fold

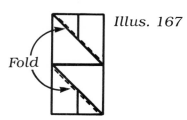

Illus. 167

Fold

Illus. 168

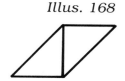

Use the other half of the sheet of paper to make a second Spinning Star section exactly like the one you just finished. The two parts to the Star each look like Illus. 168.

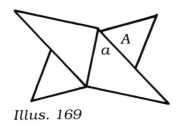

To assemble the Star, place both pieces before you so that the loose sides face up. Slip one part inside the other so that the star looks like Illus. 169. Insert point A into the little pocket formed by the folded paper on flap B.

Now work your way around the Star. Insert the four points into the four little folded pockets. When you finish Spinning Star it looks like Illus. 170.

Illus. 170

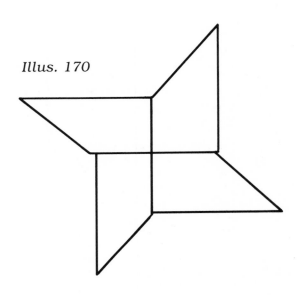

To get your Star moving, just flick one of its points hard with the end of your finger. It will go spinning across the room or across the table.

Wind Spinner

An empty milk carton can be turned into a fantastic Wind Spinner.

Make the three cuts shown in Illus. 171. Do these cuts on all four sides of the carton; therefore it does not matter which side you start with. Remember that milk cartons are extremely tough. Don't push the scissor point into yourself!

When all the cuts are made, it's time for some folding. The dotted lines in Illus. 171 show these folds. Flap A on the left is folded down, into the carton. Do this fold first on all four sides.

Illus. 171

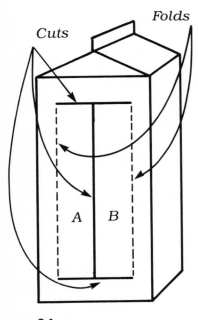

94

Next, fold flap B up so that it sticks out from the carton. Naturally, you will do all four sides in the same way so that the Wind Spinner will look like Illus. 172.

Illus. 172

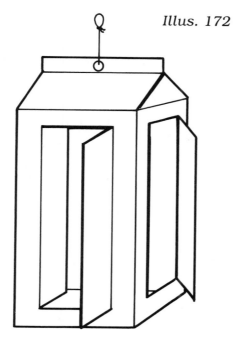

Poke a little hole in the top of the carton and tie a string into the hole as in Illus. 172. Now hold the Spinner by the string and blow gently on it. You will be surprised how little air it takes to make the Spinner turn.

If you want to make the Wind Spinner a bit fancier, tape or glue strips of foil onto the flaps which stick out from the carton. If you have some Christmas wrapping paper handy, try it instead of foil. Metallic wrapping paper makes a really flashy Wind Spinner.

Hang your Spinner near an open window, outside on the porch, or from a low tree branch. It is quite an attention getter. A bonus: When the string gets all wound up in one direction and the breeze drops, the Spinner will reverse direction as the string unwinds.

Gardeners use these Wind Spinners to frighten away birds from their plants. They may help keep birds out of fruit trees as well, when the wind is blowing.

Windmill

No one wants to throw away those wonderful round boxes that salt and oatmeal come in. Now you don't have to—make them into little windmills.

If you don't have an empty salt or oatmeal box, cut off a foot of cardboard tubing from a roll of wrapping paper.

First, decide if you want to color your Windmill or leave it saying "Salt" or "Oatmeal." If you want to put on a door and windows and give it some color, wrap a sheet of paper around the outside of the box and tape or glue it into place. Now doors and windows are no problem.

A good Windmill usually has a pointed top. That is easy as well. Cut a circle of paper from either notebook or typing paper. Construction paper works fine, too. Make this paper circle at least 8 inches across. Cut from one edge to the middle as in Illus. 173.

Illus. 173

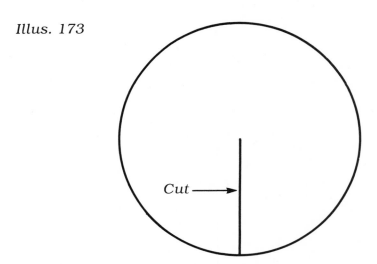

Cut ⟶

To turn this circle into a pointed roof, just slip one side of the cut edge inside the other edge. Pull the cut edges so that they overlap, and it will turn into a cone just like the one in Illus. 174.

Tape ⟶

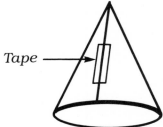

Illus. 174

The more the sides overlap, the smaller is the cone's base. Overlap the edges enough so that the cone fits the top of your carton or tube. As you can see, your circle is a "one size fits all" sort of roof.

When the roof is the proper size, tape, staple, or glue the loose sides together. Use three or four pieces of tape.

Now for the blades of the mill. Another sheet of notebook or typing paper is all you need. Make a square sheet by folding one corner over as in Illus. 175. Cut away the shaded area and unfold the square. This should make a good Windmill blade (a salt carton or a small container may need a smaller blade).

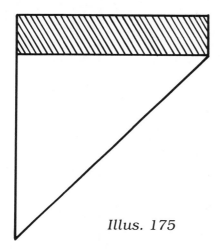

Illus. 175

Cut from each corner halfway to the middle of the square as in Illus. 176.

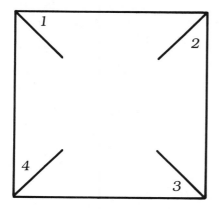

Illus. 176

Now bend (don't fold) the numbered tips to the middle of the paper. Start with corner 1 in Illus. 177, and bend the corners in order. Push a straight pin through each tip as you turn it. In fact, a tiny drop of glue on each point wouldn't hurt, either. Four tips and a pin all at once need about five hands. The glue will help. Illus. 177 shows the completed blade with the pin in place through the middle.

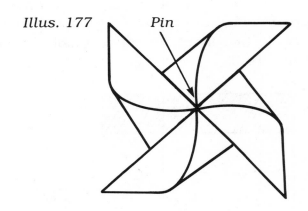

Illus. 177   Pin

Now cut a little strip of paper about ¼ × 2 inches. Roll it into a hollow tube ¼ inch long and about ⅛ inch across the hollow center. Tape or glue the loose end.

Push the pin all the way through the Windmill blade. Slide the little tube you just made onto the pin behind the blade. This little tube acts as a washer to keep the blade from hitting the Windmill.

Now push the pin into the side of the round salt or oatmeal carton and your Windmill is ready for testing. Blow on the blade. It should turn freely.

Set your Windmill near an open window and it will turn whenever a breeze blows. Or, place it near a heat vent and when the furnace blower comes on, the Windmill will turn.

Heat Spinner

This moving paper toy is a little merry-go-round which slowly turns due to the fact that hot air rises.

Begin with a sheet of thin typing paper. Tissue paper is even better, though it can be a little hard to work with. Notebook paper will do if necessary.

Draw a circle on the paper about 8 inches across. If you don't have a compass, just use an 8-inch plate or pan lid.

Make the four cuts shown in Illus. 178. In each pair of cuts the long cut is about 2½ inches long. The shorter cut should be about ½ inch long. Make certain the long cuts point right at the middle of the circle.

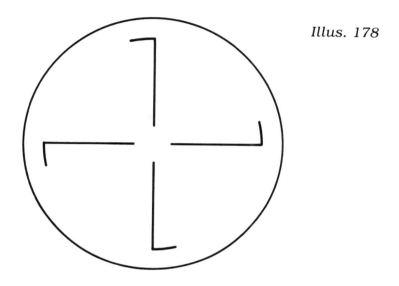

Illus. 178

These cuts form four little flaps. Bend these flaps up as in Illus. 179. Do not bend them up so far that they stand straight up. Each flap should be at about a 45° angle. If you aren't into 45° angles, bend each flap up so that it is halfway between being flat and standing straight up.

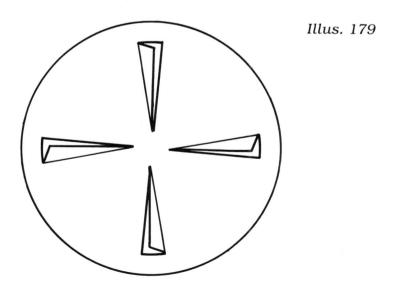

Illus. 179

Next, cut from the side of the circle to its center, as in Illus. 180. Pull the two sides of the cut together so that they overlap. As you do this the middle of the circle will rise and become a very shallow cone. Tape the two sides together as in Illus. 181.

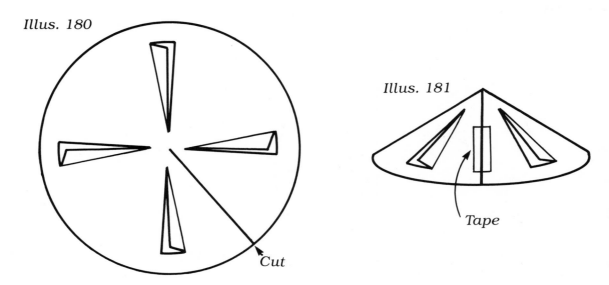

Illus. 180

Illus. 181

Tape

Cut

Now cut several strips of paper about 2 inches wide. Tape them end to end to form a long, narrow strip of about 2 feet long. This is the Heat Spinner's side.

Cut along one side of the narrow strip shown in Illus. 182. These cuts need to be ¼ inch deep. They are not spaced evenly. What you are doing is forming ½-inch tabs every 3 or 4 inches. The dotted lines between the tabs show where to fold over the paper between them so that just the tabs stick up.

Illus. 182

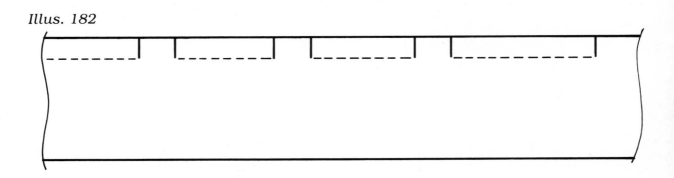

Wrap this strip around the Heat Spinner's outer edge. Use a bit of glue or a small strip of transparent tape to fasten each tab to the edge of the Heat Spinner.

This is a little heat curtain which helps direct rising hot air upwards in the Heat Spinner. Illus. 183 shows the curtain in place.

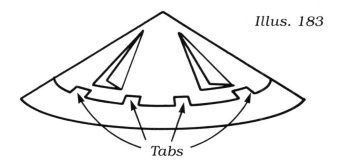

Illus. 183

Tabs

To test the Heat Spinner, balance it on the point of a pencil. This is not as hard as it sounds. Just hold the pencil at the eraser end and let the point stick into the center of the Spinner.

Now hold the Heat Spinner over a radiator or a heat vent. The rising hot air should make the Spinner turn very slowly. The thinner the paper you used, the better and faster the turn. Try holding the pencil and Spinner over a lamp. If everything is perfect, the rising hot air from the lamp will turn the Spinner.

DO NOT use the Heat Spinner with a candle or any sort of open flame, nor place it on a light bulb.

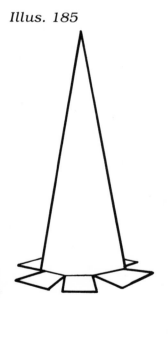

Illus. 184

Tape

Cuts

Illus. 185

If your Heat Spinner turns with the lamp's heat, you have a very fine toy indeed. You can tape the eraser end of the pencil to the metal supports at the top of the lamp or on the lamp's shade. Don't ever leave the room with the Spinner on a lamp which is turned on, though.

Most Spinners need more heat than a lamp gives off. Radiators or heat vents are usually better. In these cases a stand is needed.

Roll a sheet of notebook paper into a cone with a very sharp point, as in Illus. 184. Just roll the paper loosely at one end and tightly at the other. Fasten the loose side with a strip of tape.

Make six cuts in the base of the cone. These are shown in Illus. 184. Each cut should be about ½ inch deep. Make the cuts deeper on the side of the paper which sticks out farthest.

Fold the paper between the cuts outward. The cone should stand up as in Illus 185.

Cut a piece of heavy cardboard 4 inches square. Glue together thin layers if you don't have any heavy cardboard. Place the cone in the middle of the cardboard. Glue or tape the flaps on the bottom of the cone into place and you have a Heat Spinner stand like the one in Illus. 186.

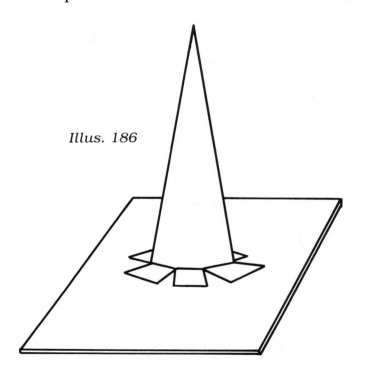

Illus. 186

If the base tips over with the Heat Spinner in place, add another layer of cardboard or put some weight on the top of the base. If you make the base larger, remember you don't want to keep the rising heat from turning the Spinner.

Color future Spinners so that they have different effects as they turn. It is easier to color them before you begin cutting.

Mobiles

There are all sorts of Mobiles—toys that move when a breeze passes by. This Mobile is a vertical mobile. It hangs straight down with each piece directly above the other.

Illus. 187 shows the basic way to assemble one of these Mobiles. A short piece of thread connects each section to the section above or below.

There is no limit to the basic shapes you can use in making your Mobile, if you remember to center the holes in the top and bottom. For some ideas check Illus. 188.

Illus. 187

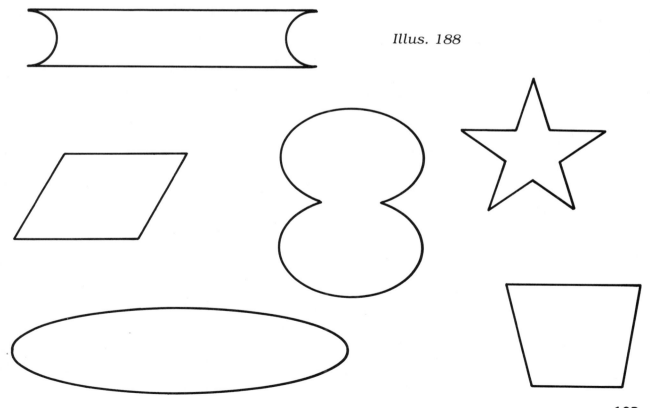

Illus. 188

103

Use any kind of material in making these toys. Construction paper, cereal box material, or pieces cut from file cards or folders are all good. For that matter, so is notebook or typing paper.

Color or paint the sections before putting the Mobile together. It is usually easier to color at least one side before cutting the Mobile piece out. Holiday wrapping paper makes extremely colorful Mobiles, especially the metallic paper. Glue or tape wrapping paper onto a base of construction paper or heavier material.

Hang the Mobile where there will be a breeze. A window or doorway is the best place, but a heat vent is also good. Even the breeze from someone walking by will make it move.

Geometric designs make great Mobiles. Illus. 189 gives you some starting ideas.

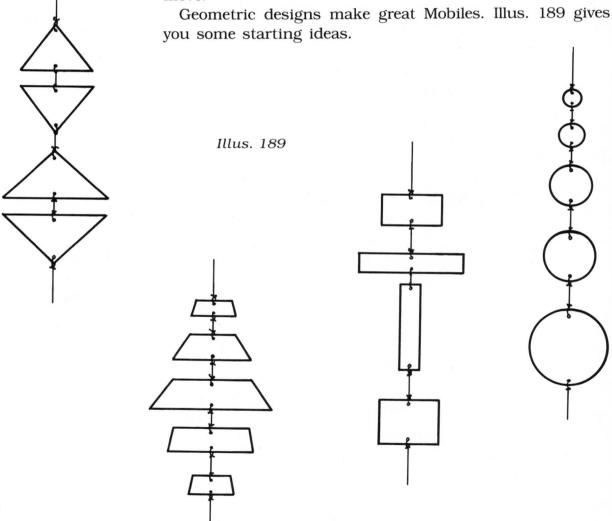

Illus. 189

Combine a variety of shapes in one Mobile. Illus. 190 shows how this can be done.

Illus. 190

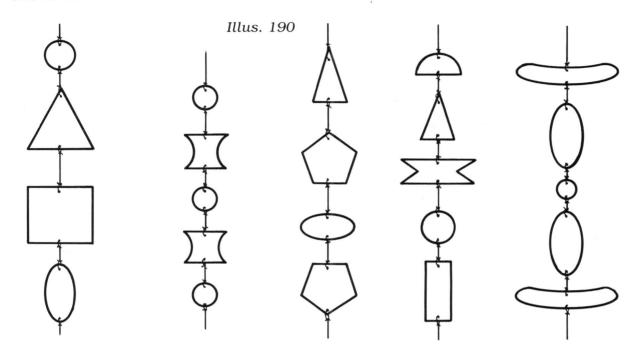

Use several layers of colored paper to give each section a different look. A few ideas are in Illus. 191.

Illus. 191

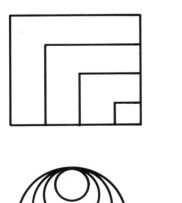

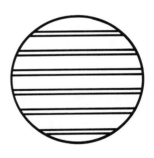

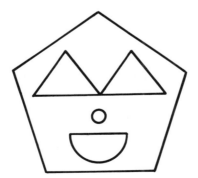

Ideas from nature such as the fish, butterflies, and owl faces in Illus. 192 make great Mobiles.

There's no limit to the number of designs you can use. The only limit you may discover will be when you run out of places to hang them.

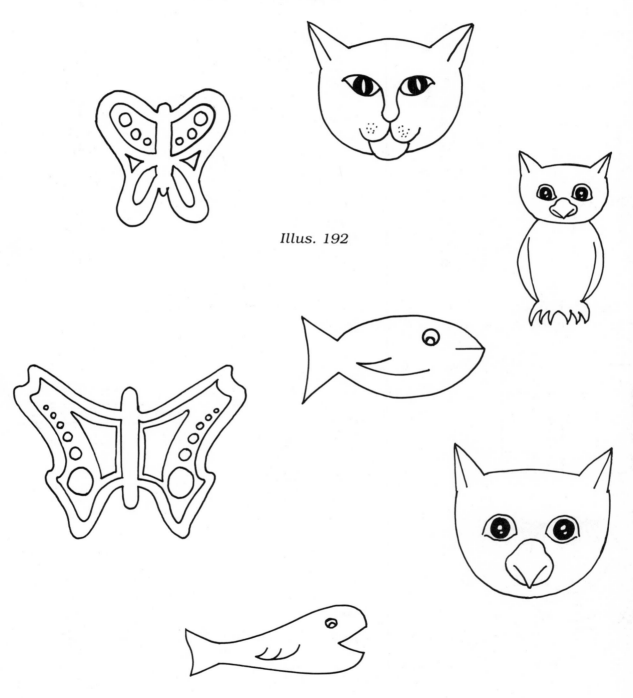

Illus. 192

· 6 ·
Toys with Wheels

It is not very hard to turn a milk carton or other small box into a toy with wheels. All it takes is a little work and some imagination.

Cart

Let's begin with a simple Cart. The little half-pint milk carton you get with your lunch at school is great. The bottom part of a regular milk carton is just as good if you can't get a smaller one. Even a small box will work if you don't have a milk carton to use. That's the great thing about making toys like these.

Cut two wheels. Wheels 2 inches or so across should do the job. If you have a compass, use it. If you don't, draw around food cans or bottle lids. Just be extremely careful poking a hole in the middle for the axle. As we have said before, don't poke your finger or the furniture.

Cut a pair of shafts for the Cart. One is pictured in Illus. 193. Make these about ¾ × 10 inches.

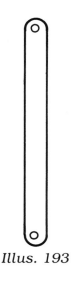

Illus. 193

Make a hole in each end of each shaft as in Illus. 193. One end will fit over the Cart's axles. The other is for a piece of string or thread to pull the Cart. Illus. 194 shows how to attach the shaft and wheel to one side of the Cart.

A paper fastener or paper clip is a good axle. (Remember how to make a paper clip into an axle, as on page 71?) If necessary, tape the long end to the inside of the Cart so that it does not work loose or wobble.

Illus. 194

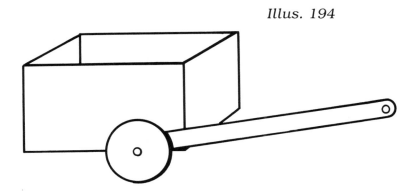

Illus. 195 shows the finished Cart. You can put a toy horse out in front and tie him to the shafts, as shown in Illus. 195. If you don't have an animal, you can pull the Cart by hand.

Illus. 195

If you want a larger cart, make one using another set of wheels so that it has four wheels instead of two. Use a quart or half-gallon milk carton and cut the carton lengthwise to make a long cart.

If you put cargo in the Cart the wheels are likely to bend. To solve the problem, make each wheel out of several thicknesses of material. Cut six wheels and glue three together to make each wheel for a two-wheeled Cart. This cutting and gluing takes a few minutes more but the wheels are much stronger.

Wheelbarrow

Turning a milk carton into a toy Wheelbarrow is not very hard at all.

Cut a milk carton or small box in half the long way. Cut two pieces of the unused milk carton material (or some old cardboard) each about 2 inches wide and 8 or more inches long.

Fold each piece in thirds the long way. The dotted lines in Illus. 196 show these folds. Use several strips of tape to fasten the folded material firmly together.

Now cut two pieces of the same material so that each piece is about 2 inches wide and 6 inches long. Fold each of these in thirds and tape them tightly so that they do not unfold.

Illus. 196

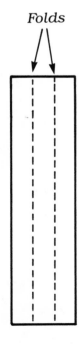

Folds

In one end of each piece carefully poke an axle hole. Make the wheel 3 inches across. Cut out three or four wheels the same size and glue them together to make one strong wheel. Carefully poke an axle hole in the center of each wheel before gluing them all together.

Illus. 197 shows how to put the Wheelbarrow together. Staple the two handles onto either side of the Wheelbarrow bed as shown. If you don't have a stapler you can use tape or glue, but staples work best on milk carton material.

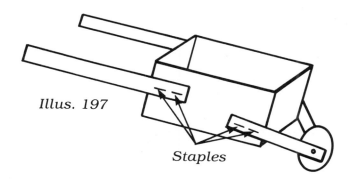

Illus. 197

Staples

Staple the shorter shaft pieces to the front of the Wheel-barrow. Be sure that you place the axle holes at the front. Slip the wheel between the shaft pieces and put in the axle. A paper fastener or paper clip makes a good axle. Just be sure the axle hole in the wheel is large enough so that the wheel can turn.

I think it's my turn!

Basic Vehicles

Milk cartons and cardboard containers allow you to make a great variety of different vehicles. Illus. 198 shows several ideas for turning milk cartons into trucks.

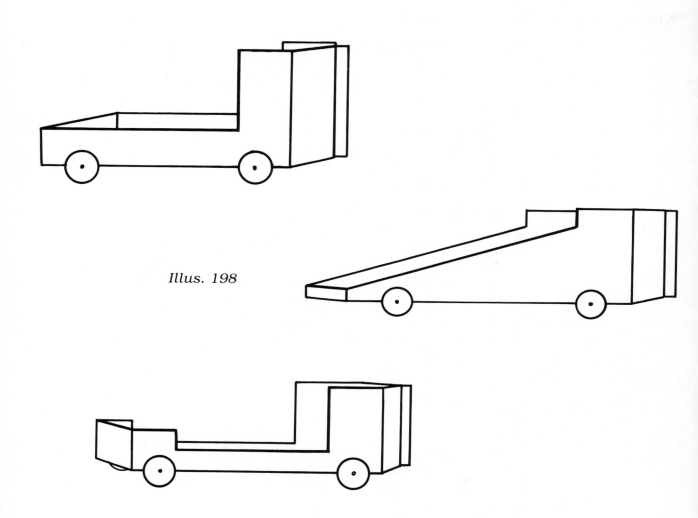

Illus. 198

The most difficult thing about wheeled vehicles is making the wheels and axles. If you have some wheels from a worn-out toy, use them. If not, keep using several layers of material just as you did for the Wheelbarrow.

When you make multi-layered wheels, remember to poke the axle hole in each layer before gluing the layers together. Even the sharpest scissor point can have trouble going through four or five layers of tough material.

Here's another idea. Cut a smaller washer out of cardboard to put on each side of the wheel. Illus. 199 shows how these washers are placed. Do *not* glue them to the wheel. Their purpose is to rub against the axle or body of the vehicle and still allow the wheel to turn. A small bead also makes a great washer.

If you use paper fasteners or bent paper clips for axles, each wheel has its own axle. To put two wheels on the same axle, make an axle housing from a plastic drinking straw.

Illus. 200 shows how the two axle housings fit through a milk carton truck.

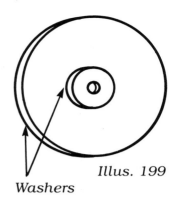

Illus. 199

Washers

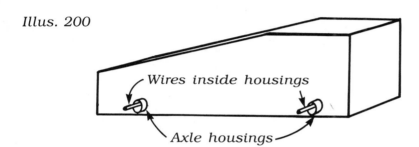

Illus. 200

Wires inside housings

Axle housings

The axle is a short length of wire. As you can see in Illus. 200, the wire axle fits inside the plastic straw housing.

Slip the wheels onto the ends of the axle and bend the axle end up. It won't hurt to put a bit of tape over the end of the axle and onto the washer. Illus. 201 gives you an idea of how to do this.

Illus. 201

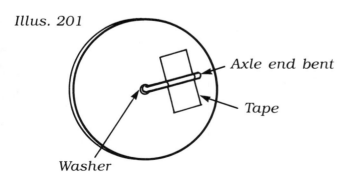

Axle end bent

Tape

Washer

Illus. 202

Another idea for wheels is corrugated paper. It's the stuff with the wavy layer glued between two smooth layers. Cut a narrow strip of corrugated paper in which the cut crosses the waves. What you end up with looks like Illus. 202.

Roll the strip tightly into a wheel like the one in Illus. 203. Glue or tape the loose end into place.

Illus. 203

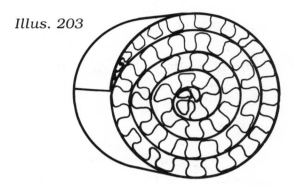

If you want to color or paint the sides of a milk carton, do the artwork on a paper and glue or tape it to the carton. It is just about impossible to draw or color on the milk carton itself. Other cartons, of course, don't have the slick surface of a milk carton and will take paint or colors.

Use your imagination and you can build a truck, a car, or if you are into frontier days, wagons!

Here's one final hint. Don't throw away wheels from your old vehicles. Save them for the new ones.

Balloon-Powered Car

Cut a milk carton to match Illus. 204. About all you should have left is one side, half of the bottom, and a little bit of two other sides to brace the bottom.

Illus. 204

Hole

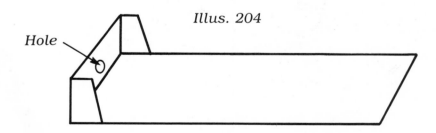

Make a hole in the carton's base, which will be the rear of the car. This hole is for the balloon's mouth to stick through. Start with a ½-inch hole, and enlarge it if necessary. The smaller the hole, the more slowly the air will escape from the balloon.

Tape two plastic drinking straws to the car for axle housings. Place these under the car as in Illus. 205.

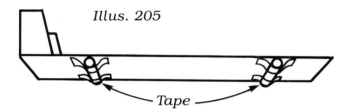

Illus. 205

Make your wheels and the axles. (If you forgot about the axles, check page 71.) Since this car won't be carrying a load, you don't need to make the wheels very thick. Two layers should do the job. Use washers or little beads on either side of each wheel.

Push the mouth of the balloon through the hole, blow the balloon up and let the car go. As the air escapes from the balloon your car should travel forward. Illus. 206 shows the car ready for its trial run.

Illus. 206

You don't need to have a safety belt for the balloon unless the hole for the balloon's mouth is too large.

The Balloon-Powered Car won't set any speed or distance records, but it is a lot of fun.

· 7 ·
Quick Games
for
Fast Fun

Hop Toad Race

How many times has either a file card or a piece cut from a cereal box been just the material needed for a project? Here is another.

Cut a Hop Toad out of the material. Illus. 207 shows a simple Hop Toad. Make your first Hop Toad 3 or 4 inches high. If you want to get fancy, color it green or grey and maybe give it some spots.

Illus. 207

Hole

Note the hole in the toad's chest in Illus. 208. Make this hole just a little above the toad's center, and make it ¼ inch across.

To finish the Hop Toad you need a piece of string about 12 feet long. Be sure there are not any knots in the string because a knot will end your Hop Toad's race right in the middle. If you don't have string, thread will work just fine.

Tie one end of the string or thread to the leg of a chair or something solid. Run the other end of the string through the hole in the toad's chest, and hold the other end tight. Place the toad about 1 foot from the string's loose end.

Now, tighten and loosen the string and move it up and down in hopping motions. Your Hop Toad will begin to advance along the string.

Make several Hop Toads, and you and your friends can hold a Hop Toad Race. Better still, make other kinds of racing creatures. Illus. 208 shows some ideas.

Illus. 208

Hole

Ring Toss

Ring Toss has been played for hundreds and probably even thousands of years. It is still as popular now as it was when your grandparents played it.

Begin with a long tube for the goal. The tube from a roll of paper towels is perfect, but the tube of a toilet-tissue roll will work as well. You could also make your own. Place two or three sheets of notebook or typing paper on top of each other. Roll them into a tube about 1 inch across. Tape the loose edges of the roll and you have a great tube.

Use a shoe box or any low cardboard box to mount your goal. Make a round hole in the lid just large enough for one end of the tube. Slip the tube through the hole. Push it through the lid about 1 inch deep. Use three or four strips of tape to fasten the tube to the box lid. Illus. 209 shows how. If the tube wants to tip to one side or the other, tape it to the top of the box lid.

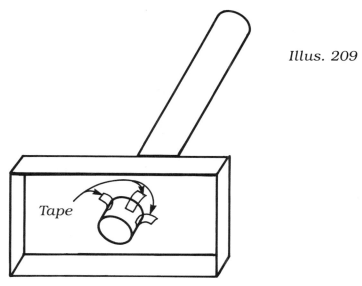

Tape

Make the rings from paper plates. Cut the center out as in Illus. 210. Fasten two or three of these rings together to make one strong ring. Fasten the layers with tape or glue.

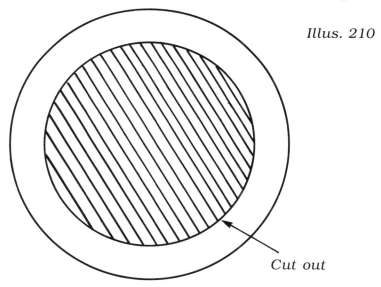

Illus. 210

Cut out

If you don't have paper plates to spare, then cut the rings from other kinds of cardboard. If you use thin cardboard, remember to make the rings three layers thick. If you use heavier cardboard, one layer may do the job. If you're unsure, give a ring a practice toss or two. Rings which are too light in weight are hard to throw accurately.

Paint or color the tube or the rings. It helps to mark the rings for each player differently so that there is no question who threw which ring.

Illus. 211 shows the completed tube and base and several ways you can paint or color the rings to make them easy to identify.

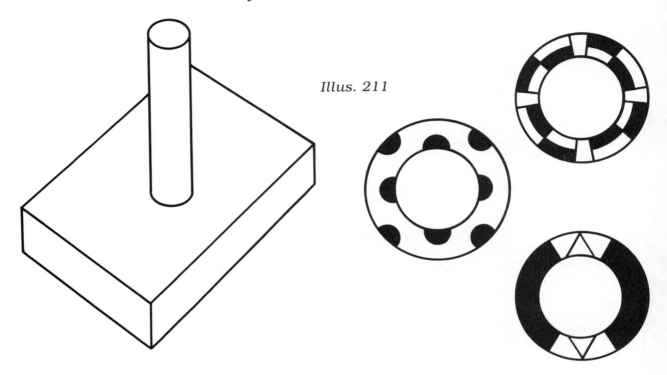

Illus. 211

To make the game of Ring Toss easier or harder, try tossing the rings from close to the target or farther away. Also, try making the rings smaller. After playing the game you may decide to try smaller rings than those you just made.

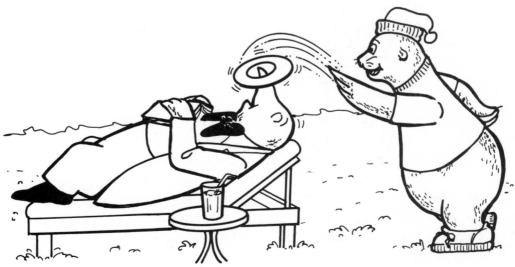

Sometimes you don't need a base!

Marble Roll

Here's a game which takes only a few minutes to build and can be played for hours and hours. You can play it against your little brother or sister, or even Dad and Mom.

Start with a shoe box, or any small box. Turn the box upside down so that the open top faces the floor. Cut five or so openings in the side of the box. One way to do this is in Illus. 212.

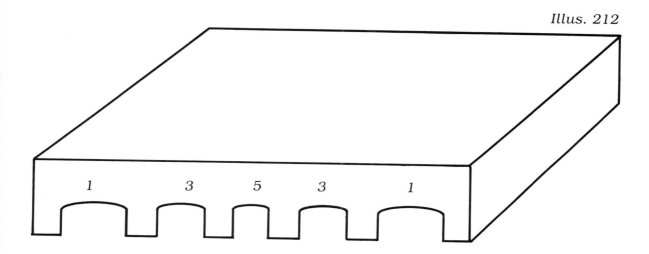

Illus. 212

Note that the width of the openings varies. The widest openings are worth one point. The narrowest opening is a five-point shot. Get it? Great! Make your first Marble Roll game with the one-point openings about 2 inches wide and the five-pointer only 1 inch wide. The three-point slots should be about 1½ inches across. Write the point values above each opening.

Five marbles per player is a good way to begin. How to take turns is up to you. Roll one at a time or roll all five at once. Count only the marbles which go inside the target. After everyone has rolled, gather up each player's marbles and go to the next round. Try playing until the winner reaches fifty; then set any score as the winning score. If two players reach fifty in the same turn, the high score wins.

The first time you play, it is a good idea to roll from only 4 or 5 feet away. It's harder than it looks! Later, you can move the starting line farther away.

Illus. 213 shows another target. Compare this one with Illus. 212 and decide which you like better. Or, come up with a target plan all your own.

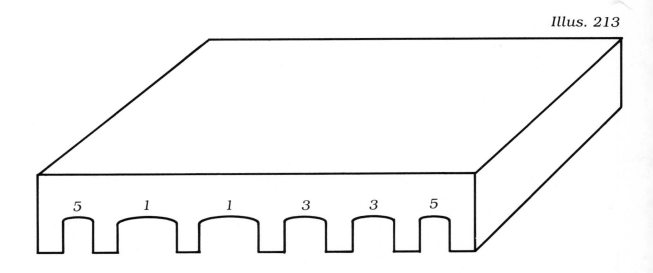

Illus. 213

Marble Bowling

It doesn't take much longer to set up Marble Bowling than it did Marble Roll.

Begin with the bottom of a box such as a soft-drink carton or a cereal box placed on its front side. Cut one end out of the box so that it looks like Illus. 214. If you are using a cereal box, cut the top side off as well.

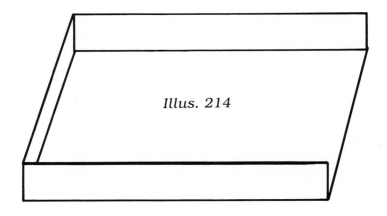

Illus. 214

Take a piece of wire as wide as the box plus 10 inches. Bend the wire so that it forms a loop or bridge from one side of the box to the other, as in Illus. 215.

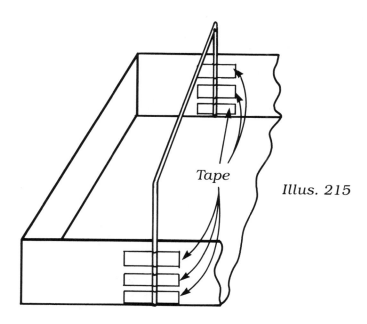

Tape

Illus. 215

If you are using a box made of thick corrugated cardboard, just push the ends of the wires into the cardboard between the layers. Use several pieces of tape (check Illus. 215) to fasten the wire ends in place if you're using a cereal box.

Now make your bowling targets. Start with three paper clips. Later, you can go on to use four or five, if you want. Now comes the tricky part. Slip the paper clips over the wire. To do this you must twist or bend each clip. Illus. 216 shows how. Be sure you twist or bend or turn the top end of the clip so that it is at right angles to the rest of the clip. Do not bend the rest of the clip out of shape, or it won't work.

Twist 90°   Illus. 216

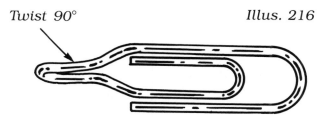

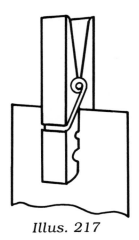

Illus. 217

If there are no paper fasteners or paper clips to be had, try wooden clothespins. Run the wire through the middle of the clothespins; then attach the wire to the box. Illus. 217 shows how.

Now make three or four target cards. Use stiff material, such as cereal box sides. They need to be just tall enough so that when the bent clip is slipped over the wire, the target can fit into the bottom of the clip and still not quite touch the bottom of the box. About 3 inches is fine. Illus. 218 shows this step.

Illus. 218

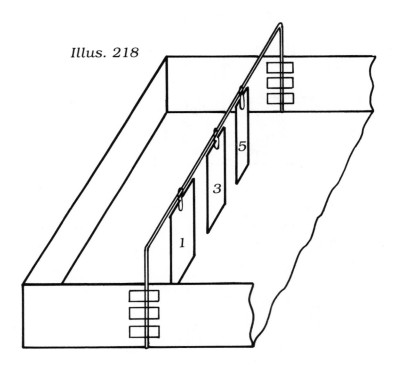

Make one target card about ½ inch wide, the next 1 inch, and the third 1½ inches. If you are using four targets it won't hurt to make the fourth one 2 inches wide. Label these targets with point values so that the widest is worth one point, the next in width two, and so on. Make the narrowest worth five points as a little extra bonus for good aim.

Each player gets three, or four, or five marbles to roll. It is up to you, as is how the turns work. To count as a point the marble must not just hit a target but actually roll under it. Glancing shots don't count.

Play to a total of fifty and play again. Just one thing about the winner: If players alternate shots, the first to reach fifty wins; but if one player rolls all at once and two players break fifty, then the high score wins.

After Marble Bowling a few times you may decide to make the game a little harder. When the marble hits the edge of the box's bottom, it often takes a wild hop and ends up somewhere other than where you hoped it would go. Illus. 219 shows how to cut part of each side of the box away. The flap which is left sticking out at the bottom can now be bent down just a bit along the dotted line. The result looks like Illus. 220. It creates a little ramp which your marbles must go up before entering the target area. This makes the game a lot harder.

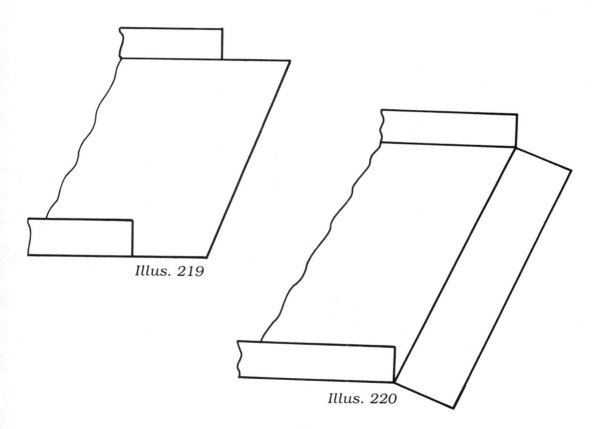

Illus. 219

Illus. 220

You can play the game with or without the ramp, with the target close or far, with wide or narrow cards, and with the cards closer or farther apart. Feel free to change the game any way you wish, to make it more fun.

Index

j745.592 Churchill, E. Richard
C   (Elmer Richard)

          Fast & funny paper
          toys you can make.

$14.95

DATE		
JY 26 '97	SE 15 08	
AG 27 98	OC 13 08	
NO 1 '97	MY 12 '09	
SE 23 '98	JY 13 '10	
SE 29 '99	DE 9 '10	
AG 8 '00		
AUG 7 2002	AG 11 11	
NOV 21 2002	JY 18 15	
SEP 22 2003		
FEB 24 2005		
JUL 11 2004		
AP 19 07		